WINE
TASTING
Journal

A LOGBOOK TO
RATE, RECORD, AND
REMEMBER WINES

DOUG PAULDING

P PETER PAUPER PRESS, INC.
WHITE PLAINS, NEW YORK

This book is dedicated to my siblings, my son, and a cousin or two. I was born into a large family and there was much chaos in our lives and in our home. We were raised as free-range kids moving and morphing and meandering through the neighborhood, on foot or on bikes, to sports events, to birthday parties, to our tiny downtown. Our daytime was often unaccounted for as most neighbors had open door policies, and there were many neighborhood kids. But my siblings and I always returned home to a sit-down family dinner, a made bed, and an immaculate home. My siblings—Peter, Bob, Betsy, Sue, Barbara, Trish, and Chris—and I share a unique relationship. We are all close friends, individually and as a group. We all share each others' triumphs and challenges. And we all love to get together over a glass, or a bottle, or a case of inspired wine. My parents, Polly and Bud, no longer of this dimension, would rejoice in this. My son, Aaron, has simply been, from the beginning, the pride of my personal world.

Images used under license from Shutterstock.com

Designed by Margaret Rubiano

Visit us at www.peterpauper.com

INTRODUCTION

S ome time ago I opened a noteworthy and moderately expensive bottle of wine with a good friend of mine, and reverting to my background as a wine reviewer for an international wine publication, I began to throw out some obvious descriptives for what we were tasting. "I'm getting dark cherry and hints of pomegranate with some black pepper notes, spice, leather, and cigar box." My friend grew tired of this quickly and said, "But can't I just say if I like it or not? This gets too complicated." Well, of course you can, but it might become impossible to replicate what you like and find a suitable and enjoyable bottle in the future. Granted, there are wine snobs who like to embellish and complicate the process of wine tasting, but let's move forward here with a guiding theme: simplicity. I enjoy carefully made and regionally inspired peasant food; unadorned, well-crafted, honest clothing that drapes naturally; and attractive jewelry without the bling. So, let's bring this concept to wine tasting and simplify.

The first question is: why describe at all? When you go into a wine store or a restaurant, the merchant or sommelier may approach you to assist. If you can tell them wines you have enjoyed or descriptives you look for, they will have a far better chance of showing you something you are almost certain to like. And as you fine-tune your palate over time by not just drinking, but by tasting with an analytical approach, better wines will find their way to you. Notable wine opportunities in my life increased in proportion to my growing tasting skills and circle of wine friends. I used to dine regularly in a beautiful restaurant in my hometown. The French owner, Joseph, would often bring me a taste of something to get my opinion. And if an expensive wine was served and refused at a table, he would bring me a taste to confirm either its soundness or its flaws. Another friend was given a case of cognac from pre-World War II. He brought out a bottle for us to taste and discuss. A memorable treat! And still another friend opened a La Tâche, one of the truly exceptional wines of the world from Burgundy's exemplary Domaine de la Romanée-Conti. We discussed the intricacies of this special wine, including the nuance and depth of flavors, and then we basked in the bouquet. It remains one of the most sublime and unforgettable moments in my wine world.

A really good place to start the process of wine appreciation is opening a bottle with a friend who has a more refined palate. Open, pour, taste, discuss. There are short courses offered up everywhere that will educate and improve your knowledge and palate. Visits to wineries, either local or while on trips, and tasting a variety of their wines will help you experience different grapes, wine styles, and blends. Wine stores often have winery representatives pouring tastes of their wines who would love to discuss their region or winery with you. And restaurants everywhere have wine and food pairing dinners with the winemaker or a winery expert guiding you through the process.

Many of the bigger cities host large regional wine tastings, often for a very reasonable fee. These tastings are often exclusively for the media in the afternoon and are opened up to the public in the evening. They will have several producers and representatives from a particular wine region. Most significant newspapers have a respectable wine writer who can give inspired advice through their columns. There are also many organizations offering multi-week wine education courses, with professional certification as a goal. You need not be in the industry to sign up for one of these courses. Join or start a wine tasting group, similar to a book club, where each week or month one person learns about a wine region, provides wines from the region, and leads the tasting. In this industry, the guided and self-guided education possibilities are endless. And, of course, everyone with an interest should begin to develop a personal wine library, for learning or for reference. *Exploring Wine* from the Culinary Institute of America is an excellent reference textbook. I use it often. Kevin Zraly's *Windows on the World Complete Wine Course* and Marnie Old's *Wine: A Tasting Course* can be read systematically cover to cover or randomly opened anywhere to improve your knowledge.

TASTING WINE

Let's simply get started. Open a bottle of wine and pour yourself a glass. And no, it doesn't have to be a special occasion to open a bottle. First, observe the **color** and appearance. Red, white, rosé, sparkling, or something else. They all show their color, vibrancy, and activity. As for color, if it's red, what shade of red? Is it translucent cherry red, like a burgundy or gamay, or is it deep, dark, and opaque, like a shiraz, a malbec, or a tannat? Is it brick red, dark red, ruby, garnet, magenta? Each could indicate a grape or perhaps a region or age. As for **appearance**, if it is white, is it mostly transparent and pale, as in an un-oaked Sauvignon Blanc, or is it golden or yellowish, like a Chardonnay? White wines gain color with age and red wines tend to lose color. Color variations of rosés are a function of the amount of time the juice has contact with the red grape skins, which can be a clue to the region. Some rosés from the Languedoc region of southern France can be so lightly colored they look like onion skin and you must hold them against a white background to even see the color, while the rosés of the Navarra region, just a few miles south in north-central Spain, are often a bright and festive translucent cherry red.

Next, give the glass a good and hearty swirl. The first drips that descend from the top of the swirl, that stream down the side of the glass, known as legs, are meaningless. But be patient. The secondary legs that fall after the primaries disappear will tell you alcohol level or sugar content. The longer these secondary legs take to start and then to descend, the higher the alcohol or sugar content. A simple sniff will tell you whether it's alcohol or sugar content. Give another good and hearty swirl and before things slow down in the glass take a big inhale. Don't be shy. Put your entire nose into the glass and take a deep sniff. There should be all kinds of aromas and potential flavors enticing you to taste. These **aromas**, known as the nose of the wine, might initially be difficult to attach a name or descriptor to. By tasting with folks with more wine experience, or by tasting with an aroma wheel and looking to see where the words match what you are experiencing, or even by reading the bottle or website for flavors to expect, you will begin to think and talk wine. (Caveat emptor: Some websites or bottle portrayals of simple wines might tend to be overly ambitious and focused more on selling the wine than providing accurate flavor descriptives.) **The Wine Aroma Wheel** (see pages 12-13) will essentially make identifying aromas and tastes a multiple-choice game with further descriptive refinements as you move from the middle of the wheel to the periphery.

And now it's time to **taste**. Take a thimble-size taste of wine into your mouth and push it around with your tongue, breathe over it, push it around some more, and let the flavors saturate your mouth. Try to isolate and identify the dominant flavors. Are you getting dark fruit, as in blackberry, or red fruit, as in fresh red cherries? Or are you getting grapefruit, lemon, or orange? Are the acids, which can be experienced on the tongue or in the salivary glands, pronounced and puckery or inconsequential?

Wine can be very dry and still be quite fruity. Winemakers will stop the fermentation process when they achieve the flavors they want. Generally, less fermentation produces more sweetness. With a longer or complete fermentation, sugars may be greatly reduced (dry), but the wine can be extremely fruity. Examples of dry but fruity wines include Sauvignon

Blanc, which often tastes citrusy but not sweet, and Bordeaux, which exudes a rich fruitiness but is likewise dry. I have tasted wonderful wines all over the **dry/sweet spectrum**. There is a situation or a food to accompany well-made wines of any level of sweetness.

Body is the impression of the weight and size of wine. A full-bodied wine seems heavier in the mouth, while a light-bodied wine slips easily across the palate.

Acids give substance, structure, length, and **balance** to the body of the wine. Without proper acidity the wine will "fall apart" and not last on the palate or on the shelf. Is there staying power in the mouth? Does it linger or vanish? Is there a textural quality, like a cottony, creamy, buttery, or honey feel on the gums and tongue? Textures in a wine will allow for length on the **finish**. The finish will be experiential. How long can you still taste and feel the wine in your mouth? Well-made wines tend to have more structure and layers and will still be present, sometimes long after the swallow. A short finish can disappear just post swallow. Wines with a long finish can last up to a minute or more. Now taste it again. And again. And again.

Making wine is as old as recorded history and has been enjoyed all over the world for two main reasons. The church and the Roman empire were growing their respective influence worldwide. The church planted grapes and made wine for ritualistic purposes and the Romans planted grapes wherever they went because wine was safe to drink, while the local available water was often contaminated by human or animal activity and could make people sick. Wine and beer became the beverage of choice because fermentation made the liquid safe. And of course, over the centuries and around the world, many other cultures and civilizations contributed to the spread of the fruit of the vine.

USING THIS JOURNAL

I have arranged this wine tasting journal as a simple diary for the wines you get to experience. Each page is organized clearly and methodically. The hope is that, with little time dedicated, you can start to see patterns develop of where you are in the wine taster continuum; that is, which grapes you prefer, what winemaking styles you prefer, and which regions and grapes of the world will likely hold your attention.

Each fill-in Tasting page features identifying prompts (wine, vintage, etc.) and descriptive prompts (color, body, etc.), and four 10-point scales. Use the first two scales to rate dryness/sweetness and balance. The third is your overall subjective tasting experience. How did the wine measure up? The fourth is a price-to-value ratio rating, which for me is key. Anyone can pick a delicious $100 wine from a wine list. The secret of choosing well and impressing your dinner mates is finding a tasty wine that overdelivers for the price. I sometimes look for underappreciated or emerging wine regions or relatively unknown grapes where attractive pricing has to be employed. And there is nothing wrong with asking a knowledgeable server or sommelier for assistance. I have asked a wine steward to pick a wine for my table that will enhance my meal and costs around $60. He went to the cellar, returned with a bottle and told me, "This is the last bottle of a case we had, drinks beautifully and was on our list at $82 but you can have it for $60." This journal will help you to find a compatible and wonderful wine for any occasion.

Improving your knowledge of wine is not just to increase your chances for finding attractive wines in the future. It's also fun. Be open-minded. I have heard friends say, "I don't like Chardonnay. It's too oaky." Or "I don't like Riesling. It's too sweet." Don't indict a grape for one bad experience. I have tasted Chardonnay in its unoaked and fruit-driven nakedness and then as a buttery, clumsily over-oaked wine, and everything in between. And Rieslings can be anywhere on the sweet-dry spectrum. Some Rieslings have a sweetness scale on the back of the bottle which will give a solid clue about what to expect.

Today is the most exciting time in history to be exploring the world of wine. Winemakers are highly trained and often university educated and come to their profession with a vast world of knowledge. They will often work in other wineries or other countries or continents before they settle in somewhere. The internet allows for knowledge and information sharing worldwide. Agronomists, winemakers, and the public are demanding better made and more natural wines. Organic, biodynamic, and earth-friendly are relatively new terms in the wine world. In the vineyard, introducing natural predators and insects to keep damaging creatures away makes for a cleaner and safer wine. And the internet allows for a dialogue possibly with the winemaker or winery. If you have a noteworthy wine experience, those responsible for crafting the wine might love to hear from you. An earnest email could get you additional information, attractive pricing for direct sales, and maybe an invitation to the winery. There's no better time than now!

WINE AROMA WHEEL

Originally created in the 1980s, and later revised, by Ann C. Noble at the University of California, Davis, the Wine Aroma Wheel has helped categorize and codify wine tasting, adding a degree of objectivity to evaluating a wine.

As A. C. Noble writes, "The quickest way to learn to recognize aromas of wine is to select two or more wines which are very different in flavor and look at the inner tier of the wheel for the words which best describe the flavor, such as Fruity or Spicy, then go to the two outside tiers for suggestions for more specific notes, such as Berry and if possible, even more specifically, Strawberry."

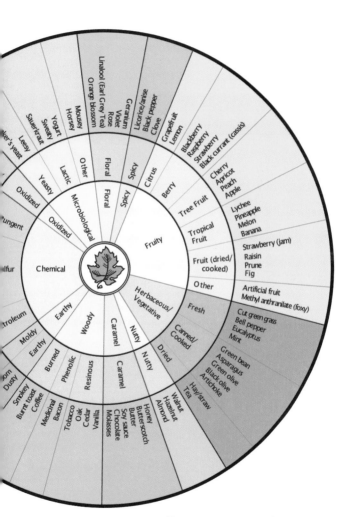

13

WINE:		Vintage:	Producer:
Region/Country:		Price:	Date Tasted:
Grape(s):			
Importer/Distributor:			Alcohol %

CIRCLE YOUR RATINGS BELOW.

Color/Style: Red   White   Rosé   Sparkling   Effervescent   Fortified

Appearance: Thin   Translucent   Saturated   Opaque

Dry/Sweet Spectrum: Dry   1   2   3   4   5   6   7   8   9   10   Sweet

Body: Light   Light to Medium   Medium   Medium to Full   Full

Balance: Unbalanced   1   2   3   4   5   6   7   8   9   10   Balanced

Finish: Short   Short to Medium   Medium   Medium to Long   Long

Overall Tasting Experience: Poor   1   2   3   4   5   6   7   8   9   10   Excellent

Price-to-Value Ratio: Poor   1   2   3   4   5   6   7   8   9   10   Excellent

Aromas and Tastes:

Comments on Vintage, Region, Winemaker:

| Recommended | | Not Recommended |
| | *(Circle One)* | |

WINE: _____ Vintage: _____ Producer: _____

Region/Country: _____ Price: _____ Date Tasted: _____

Grape(s): _____

Importer/Distributor: _____ Alcohol % _____

CIRCLE YOUR RATINGS BELOW.

Color/Style: Red   White   Rosé   Sparkling   Effervescent   Fortified

Appearance: Thin   Translucent   Saturated   Opaque

Dry/Sweet Spectrum: Dry   1   2   3   4   5   6   7   8   9   10   Sweet

Body: Light   Light to Medium   Medium   Medium to Full   Full

Balance: Unbalanced   1   2   3   4   5   6   7   8   9   10   Balanced

Finish: Short   Short to Medium   Medium   Medium to Long   Long

Overall Tasting Experience: Poor   1   2   3   4   5   6   7   8   9   10   Excellent

Price-to-Value Ratio: Poor   1   2   3   4   5   6   7   8   9   10   Excellent

Aromas and Tastes: _____

_____

Comments on Vintage, Region, Winemaker: _____

_____

Recommended   Not Recommended
                    (Circle One)

15

WINE: _____ Vintage: _____ Producer: _____

Region/Country: _____ Price: _____ Date Tasted: _____

Grape(s): _____

Importer/Distributor: _____ Alcohol % _____

CIRCLE YOUR RATINGS BELOW.

Color/Style: Red White Rosé Sparkling Effervescent Fortified

Appearance: Thin Translucent Saturated Opaque

Dry/Sweet Spectrum: Dry 1 2 3 4 5 6 7 8 9 10 Sweet

Body: Light Light to Medium Medium Medium to Full Full

Balance: Unbalanced 1 2 3 4 5 6 7 8 9 10 Balanced

Finish: Short Short to Medium Medium Medium to Long Long

Overall Tasting Experience: Poor 1 2 3 4 5 6 7 8 9 10 Excellent

Price-to-Value Ratio: Poor 1 2 3 4 5 6 7 8 9 10 Excellent

Aromas and Tastes: _____

_____

Comments on Vintage, Region, Winemaker: _____

_____

Recommended   Not Recommended

(Circle One)

16

WINE:		Vintage:	Producer:

Region/Country: _____ Price: _____ Date Tasted: _____

Grape(s): _____

Importer/Distributor: _____ Alcohol % _____

CIRCLE YOUR RATINGS BELOW.

Color/Style: Red   White   Rosé   Sparkling   Effervescent   Fortified

Appearance: Thin   Translucent   Saturated   Opaque

Dry/Sweet Spectrum: Dry   1   2   3   4   5   6   7   8   9   10   Sweet

Body: Light   Light to Medium   Medium   Medium to Full   Full

Balance: Unbalanced   1   2   3   4   5   6   7   8   9   10   Balanced

Finish: Short   Short to Medium   Medium   Medium to Long   Long

Overall Tasting Experience: Poor   1   2   3   4   5   6   7   8   9   10   Excellent

Price-to-Value Ratio: Poor   1   2   3   4   5   6   7   8   9   10   Excellent

Aromas and Tastes: _____

_____

Comments on Vintage, Region, Winemaker: _____

_____

Recommended	Not Recommended
	(Circle One)	

WINE: _____ Vintage: _____ Producer: _____

Region/Country: _____ Price: _____ Date Tasted: _____

Grape(s): _____

Importer/Distributor: _____ Alcohol % _____

CIRCLE YOUR RATINGS BELOW.

Color/Style: Red White Rosé Sparkling Effervescent Fortified

Appearance: Thin Translucent Saturated Opaque

Dry/Sweet Spectrum: Dry 1 2 3 4 5 6 7 8 9 10 Sweet

Body: Light Light to Medium Medium Medium to Full Full

Balance: Unbalanced 1 2 3 4 5 6 7 8 9 10 Balanced

Finish: Short Short to Medium Medium Medium to Long Long

Overall Tasting Experience: Poor 1 2 3 4 5 6 7 8 9 10 Excellent

Price-to-Value Ratio: Poor 1 2 3 4 5 6 7 8 9 10 Excellent

Aromas and Tastes: _____

_____

Comments on Vintage, Region, Winemaker: _____

_____

Recommended	Not Recommended
	(*Circle One*)	

18

WINE: _____ Vintage: _____ Producer: _____

Region/Country: _____ Price: _____ Date Tasted: _____

Grape(s): _____

Importer/Distributor: _____ Alcohol % _____

CIRCLE YOUR RATINGS BELOW.

Color/Style: Red White Rosé Sparkling Effervescent Fortified

Appearance: Thin Translucent Saturated Opaque

Dry/Sweet Spectrum: Dry 1 2 3 4 5 6 7 8 9 10 Sweet

Body: Light Light to Medium Medium Medium to Full Full

Balance: Unbalanced 1 2 3 4 5 6 7 8 9 10 Balanced

Finish: Short Short to Medium Medium Medium to Long Long

Overall Tasting Experience: Poor 1 2 3 4 5 6 7 8 9 10 Excellent

Price-to-Value Ratio: Poor 1 2 3 4 5 6 7 8 9 10 Excellent

Aromas and Tastes: _____

_____

Comments on Vintage, Region, Winemaker: _____

_____

Recommended	Not Recommended
	(Circle One)	

WINE: _____ Vintage: _____ Producer: _____

Region/Country: _____ Price: _____ Date Tasted: _____

Grape(s): _____

Importer/Distributor: _____ Alcohol % _____

CIRCLE YOUR RATINGS BELOW.

Color/Style: Red White Rosé Sparkling Effervescent Fortified

Appearance: Thin Translucent Saturated Opaque

Dry/Sweet Spectrum: Dry 1 2 3 4 5 6 7 8 9 10 Sweet

Body: Light Light to Medium Medium Medium to Full Full

Balance: Unbalanced 1 2 3 4 5 6 7 8 9 10 Balanced

Finish: Short Short to Medium Medium Medium to Long Long

Overall Tasting Experience: Poor 1 2 3 4 5 6 7 8 9 10 Excellent

Price-to-Value Ratio: Poor 1 2 3 4 5 6 7 8 9 10 Excellent

Aromas and Tastes: _____

_____

Comments on Vintage, Region, Winemaker: _____

_____

Recommended	Not Recommended
	(*Circle One*)	

WINE: _____ Vintage: _____ Producer: _____

Region/Country: _____ Price: _____ Date Tasted: _____

Grape(s): _____

Importer/Distributor: _____ Alcohol % _____

CIRCLE YOUR RATINGS BELOW.

Color/Style: Red   White   Rosé   Sparkling   Effervescent   Fortified

Appearance: Thin   Translucent   Saturated   Opaque

Dry/Sweet Spectrum: Dry   1   2   3   4   5   6   7   8   9   10   Sweet

Body: Light   Light to Medium   Medium   Medium to Full   Full

Balance: Unbalanced   1   2   3   4   5   6   7   8   9   10   Balanced

Finish: Short   Short to Medium   Medium   Medium to Long   Long

Overall Tasting Experience: Poor   1   2   3   4   5   6   7   8   9   10   Excellent

Price-to-Value Ratio: Poor   1   2   3   4   5   6   7   8   9   10   Excellent

Aromas and Tastes: _____

_____

Comments on Vintage, Region, Winemaker: _____

_____

Recommended   Not Recommended

(*Circle One*)

WINE: _____ Vintage: _____ Producer: _____

Region/Country: _____ Price: _____ Date Tasted: _____

Grape(s): _____

Importer/Distributor: _____ Alcohol % _____

CIRCLE YOUR RATINGS BELOW.

Color/Style: Red White Rosé Sparkling Effervescent Fortified

Appearance: Thin Translucent Saturated Opaque

Dry/Sweet Spectrum: Dry 1 2 3 4 5 6 7 8 9 10 Sweet

Body: Light Light to Medium Medium Medium to Full Full

Balance: Unbalanced 1 2 3 4 5 6 7 8 9 10 Balanced

Finish: Short Short to Medium Medium Medium to Long Long

Overall Tasting Experience: Poor 1 2 3 4 5 6 7 8 9 10 Excellent

Price-to-Value Ratio: Poor 1 2 3 4 5 6 7 8 9 10 Excellent

Aromas and Tastes: _____

_____

Comments on Vintage, Region, Winemaker: _____

_____

Recommended   Not Recommended
                  (Circle One)

22

WINE: _____ Vintage: _____ Producer: _____

Region/Country: _____ Price: _____ Date Tasted: _____

Grape(s): _____

Importer/Distributor: _____ Alcohol % _____

CIRCLE YOUR RATINGS BELOW.

Color/Style: Red White Rosé Sparkling Effervescent Fortified

Appearance: Thin Translucent Saturated Opaque

Dry/Sweet Spectrum: Dry 1 2 3 4 5 6 7 8 9 10 Sweet

Body: Light Light to Medium Medium Medium to Full Full

Balance: Unbalanced 1 2 3 4 5 6 7 8 9 10 Balanced

Finish: Short Short to Medium Medium Medium to Long Long

Overall Tasting Experience: Poor 1 2 3 4 5 6 7 8 9 10 Excellent

Price-to-Value Ratio: Poor 1 2 3 4 5 6 7 8 9 10 Excellent

Aromas and Tastes: _____

_____

Comments on Vintage, Region, Winemaker: _____

_____

Recommended   Not Recommended

(Circle One)

23

WINE: _____ Vintage: _____ Producer: _____

Region/Country: _____ Price: _____ Date Tasted: _____

Grape(s): _____

Importer/Distributor: _____ Alcohol % _____

CIRCLE YOUR RATINGS BELOW.

Color/Style: Red   White   Rosé   Sparkling   Effervescent   Fortified

Appearance: Thin   Translucent   Saturated   Opaque

Dry/Sweet Spectrum: Dry   1   2   3   4   5   6   7   8   9   10   Sweet

Body: Light   Light to Medium   Medium   Medium to Full   Full

Balance: Unbalanced   1   2   3   4   5   6   7   8   9   10   Balanced

Finish: Short   Short to Medium   Medium   Medium to Long   Long

Overall Tasting Experience: Poor   1   2   3   4   5   6   7   8   9   10   Excellent

Price-to-Value Ratio: Poor   1   2   3   4   5   6   7   8   9   10   Excellent

Aromas and Tastes: _____

_____

Comments on Vintage, Region, Winemaker: _____

_____

Recommended	Not Recommended

(*Circle One*)

WINE: _____ Vintage: _____ Producer: _____

Region/Country: _____ Price: _____ Date Tasted: _____

Grape(s): _____

Importer/Distributor: _____ Alcohol % _____

CIRCLE YOUR RATINGS BELOW.

Color/Style: Red   White   Rosé   Sparkling   Effervescent   Fortified

Appearance: Thin   Translucent   Saturated   Opaque

Dry/Sweet Spectrum: Dry   1   2   3   4   5   6   7   8   9   10   Sweet

Body: Light   Light to Medium   Medium   Medium to Full   Full

Balance: Unbalanced   1   2   3   4   5   6   7   8   9   10   Balanced

Finish: Short   Short to Medium   Medium   Medium to Long   Long

Overall Tasting Experience: Poor   1   2   3   4   5   6   7   8   9   10   Excellent

Price-to-Value Ratio: Poor   1   2   3   4   5   6   7   8   9   10   Excellent

Aromas and Tastes: _____

_____

Comments on Vintage, Region, Winemaker: _____

_____

Recommended   Not Recommended
                    (Circle One)

WINE: _____ Vintage: _____ Producer: _____

Region/Country: _____ Price: _____ Date Tasted: _____

Grape(s): _____

Importer/Distributor: _____ Alcohol % _____

CIRCLE YOUR RATINGS BELOW.

Color/Style: Red   White   Rosé   Sparkling   Effervescent   Fortified

Appearance: Thin   Translucent   Saturated   Opaque

Dry/Sweet Spectrum: Dry   1   2   3   4   5   6   7   8   9   10   Sweet

Body: Light   Light to Medium   Medium   Medium to Full   Full

Balance: Unbalanced   1   2   3   4   5   6   7   8   9   10   Balanced

Finish: Short   Short to Medium   Medium   Medium to Long   Long

Overall Tasting Experience: Poor   1   2   3   4   5   6   7   8   9   10   Excellent

Price-to-Value Ratio: Poor   1   2   3   4   5   6   7   8   9   10   Excellent

Aromas and Tastes: _____

_____

Comments on Vintage, Region, Winemaker: _____

_____

Recommended	Not Recommended

(Circle One)

WINE: _____ Vintage: _____ Producer: _____

Region/Country: _____ Price: _____ Date Tasted: _____

Grape(s): _____

Importer/Distributor: _____ Alcohol % _____

CIRCLE YOUR RATINGS BELOW.

Color/Style: Red White Rosé Sparkling Effervescent Fortified

Appearance: Thin Translucent Saturated Opaque

Dry/Sweet Spectrum: Dry 1 2 3 4 5 6 7 8 9 10 Sweet

Body: Light Light to Medium Medium Medium to Full Full

Balance: Unbalanced 1 2 3 4 5 6 7 8 9 10 Balanced

Finish: Short Short to Medium Medium Medium to Long Long

Overall Tasting Experience: Poor 1 2 3 4 5 6 7 8 9 10 Excellent

Price-to-Value Ratio: Poor 1 2 3 4 5 6 7 8 9 10 Excellent

Aromas and Tastes: _____

_____

Comments on Vintage, Region, Winemaker: _____

_____

Recommended   Not Recommended
                (Circle One)

WINE: _____ Vintage: _____ Producer: _____

Region/Country: _____ Price: _____ Date Tasted: _____

Grape(s): _____

Importer/Distributor: _____ Alcohol % _____

CIRCLE YOUR RATINGS BELOW.

Color/Style: Red White Rosé Sparkling Effervescent Fortified

Appearance: Thin Translucent Saturated Opaque

Dry/Sweet Spectrum: Dry 1 2 3 4 5 6 7 8 9 10 Sweet

Body: Light Light to Medium Medium Medium to Full Full

Balance: Unbalanced 1 2 3 4 5 6 7 8 9 10 Balanced

Finish: Short Short to Medium Medium Medium to Long Long

Overall Tasting Experience: Poor 1 2 3 4 5 6 7 8 9 10 Excellent

Price-to-Value Ratio: Poor 1 2 3 4 5 6 7 8 9 10 Excellent

Aromas and Tastes: _____

_____

Comments on Vintage, Region, Winemaker: _____

_____

Recommended   Not Recommended
             (*Circle One*)

WINE: _____ Vintage: _____ Producer: _____

Region/Country: _____ Price: _____ Date Tasted: _____

Grape(s): _____

Importer/Distributor: _____ Alcohol % _____

CIRCLE YOUR RATINGS BELOW.

Color/Style: Red White Rosé Sparkling Effervescent Fortified

Appearance: Thin Translucent Saturated Opaque

Dry/Sweet Spectrum: Dry 1 2 3 4 5 6 7 8 9 10 Sweet

Body: Light Light to Medium Medium Medium to Full Full

Balance: Unbalanced 1 2 3 4 5 6 7 8 9 10 Balanced

Finish: Short Short to Medium Medium Medium to Long Long

Overall Tasting Experience: Poor 1 2 3 4 5 6 7 8 9 10 Excellent

Price-to-Value Ratio: Poor 1 2 3 4 5 6 7 8 9 10 Excellent

Aromas and Tastes: _____

_____

Comments on Vintage, Region, Winemaker: _____

_____

Recommended   Not Recommended
                    (*Circle One*)

WINE: _____ Vintage: _____ Producer: _____

Region/Country: _____ Price: _____ Date Tasted: _____

Grape(s): _____

Importer/Distributor: _____ Alcohol % _____

CIRCLE YOUR RATINGS BELOW.

Color/Style: Red White Rosé Sparkling Effervescent Fortified

Appearance: Thin Translucent Saturated Opaque

Dry/Sweet Spectrum: Dry 1 2 3 4 5 6 7 8 9 10 Sweet

Body: Light Light to Medium Medium Medium to Full Full

Balance: Unbalanced 1 2 3 4 5 6 7 8 9 10 Balanced

Finish: Short Short to Medium Medium Medium to Long Long

Overall Tasting Experience: Poor 1 2 3 4 5 6 7 8 9 10 Excellent

Price-to-Value Ratio: Poor 1 2 3 4 5 6 7 8 9 10 Excellent

Aromas and Tastes: _____

_____

Comments on Vintage, Region, Winemaker: _____

_____

Recommended   Not Recommended
                    (Circle One)

30

WINE: _____ Vintage: _____ Producer: _____

Region/Country: _____ Price: _____ Date Tasted: _____

Grape(s): _____

Importer/Distributor: _____ Alcohol % _____

CIRCLE YOUR RATINGS BELOW.

Color/Style: Red White Rosé Sparkling Effervescent Fortified

Appearance: Thin Translucent Saturated Opaque

Dry/Sweet Spectrum: Dry 1 2 3 4 5 6 7 8 9 10 Sweet

Body: Light Light to Medium Medium Medium to Full Full

Balance: Unbalanced 1 2 3 4 5 6 7 8 9 10 Balanced

Finish: Short Short to Medium Medium Medium to Long Long

Overall Tasting Experience: Poor 1 2 3 4 5 6 7 8 9 10 Excellent

Price-to-Value Ratio: Poor 1 2 3 4 5 6 7 8 9 10 Excellent

Aromas and Tastes: _____

_____

Comments on Vintage, Region, Winemaker: _____

_____

Recommended		Not Recommended
	(Circle One)	

WINE: _____ Vintage: _____ Producer: _____

Region/Country: _____ Price: _____ Date Tasted: _____

Grape(s): _____

Importer/Distributor: _____ Alcohol % _____

CIRCLE YOUR RATINGS BELOW.

Color/Style: Red   White   Rosé   Sparkling   Effervescent   Fortified

Appearance: Thin   Translucent   Saturated   Opaque

Dry/Sweet Spectrum: Dry   1   2   3   4   5   6   7   8   9   10   Sweet

Body: Light   Light to Medium   Medium   Medium to Full   Full

Balance: Unbalanced   1   2   3   4   5   6   7   8   9   10   Balanced

Finish: Short   Short to Medium   Medium   Medium to Long   Long

Overall Tasting Experience: Poor   1   2   3   4   5   6   7   8   9   10   Excellent

Price-to-Value Ratio: Poor   1   2   3   4   5   6   7   8   9   10   Excellent

Aromas and Tastes: _____

_____

Comments on Vintage, Region, Winemaker: _____

_____

Recommended   Not Recommended

(Circle One)

WINE: _____ Vintage: _____ Producer: _____

Region/Country: _____ Price: _____ Date Tasted: _____

Grape(s): _____

Importer/Distributor: _____ Alcohol % _____

CIRCLE YOUR RATINGS BELOW.

Color/Style: Red White Rosé Sparkling Effervescent Fortified

Appearance: Thin Translucent Saturated Opaque

Dry/Sweet Spectrum: Dry 1 2 3 4 5 6 7 8 9 10 Sweet

Body: Light Light to Medium Medium Medium to Full Full

Balance: Unbalanced 1 2 3 4 5 6 7 8 9 10 Balanced

Finish: Short Short to Medium Medium Medium to Long Long

Overall Tasting Experience: Poor 1 2 3 4 5 6 7 8 9 10 Excellent

Price-to-Value Ratio: Poor 1 2 3 4 5 6 7 8 9 10 Excellent

Aromas and Tastes: _____

_____

Comments on Vintage, Region, Winemaker: _____

_____

Recommended	Not Recommended
	(Circle One)	

WINE: _____ Vintage: _____ Producer: _____

Region/Country: _____ Price: _____ Date Tasted: _____

Grape(s): _____

Importer/Distributor: _____ Alcohol % _____

CIRCLE YOUR RATINGS BELOW.

Color/Style: Red   White   Rosé   Sparkling   Effervescent   Fortified

Appearance: Thin   Translucent   Saturated   Opaque

Dry/Sweet Spectrum: Dry   1   2   3   4   5   6   7   8   9   10   Sweet

Body: Light   Light to Medium   Medium   Medium to Full   Full

Balance: Unbalanced   1   2   3   4   5   6   7   8   9   10   Balanced

Finish: Short   Short to Medium   Medium   Medium to Long   Long

Overall Tasting Experience: Poor   1   2   3   4   5   6   7   8   9   10   Excellent

Price-to-Value Ratio: Poor   1   2   3   4   5   6   7   8   9   10   Excellent

Aromas and Tastes: _____

_____

Comments on Vintage, Region, Winemaker: _____

_____

Recommended		Not Recommended
	(Circle One)	

WINE: .... Vintage: .... Producer: ....

Region/Country: .... Price: .... Date Tasted: ....

Grape(s): ....

Importer/Distributor: .... Alcohol % ....

CIRCLE YOUR RATINGS BELOW.

Color/Style: Red White Rosé Sparkling Effervescent Fortified

Appearance: Thin Translucent Saturated Opaque

Dry/Sweet Spectrum: Dry 1 2 3 4 5 6 7 8 9 10 Sweet

Body: Light Light to Medium Medium Medium to Full Full

Balance: Unbalanced 1 2 3 4 5 6 7 8 9 10 Balanced

Finish: Short Short to Medium Medium Medium to Long Long

Overall Tasting Experience: Poor 1 2 3 4 5 6 7 8 9 10 Excellent

Price-to-Value Ratio: Poor 1 2 3 4 5 6 7 8 9 10 Excellent

Aromas and Tastes: ....

....

Comments on Vintage, Region, Winemaker: ....

....

Recommended	Not Recommended
	(Circle One)

WINE: _____ Vintage: _____ Producer: _____

Region/Country: _____ Price: _____ Date Tasted: _____

Grape(s): _____

Importer/Distributor: _____ Alcohol % _____

CIRCLE YOUR RATINGS BELOW.

Color/Style: Red White Rosé Sparkling Effervescent Fortified

Appearance: Thin Translucent Saturated Opaque

Dry/Sweet Spectrum: Dry 1 2 3 4 5 6 7 8 9 10 Sweet

Body: Light Light to Medium Medium Medium to Full Full

Balance: Unbalanced 1 2 3 4 5 6 7 8 9 10 Balanced

Finish: Short Short to Medium Medium Medium to Long Long

Overall Tasting Experience: Poor 1 2 3 4 5 6 7 8 9 10 Excellent

Price-to-Value Ratio: Poor 1 2 3 4 5 6 7 8 9 10 Excellent

Aromas and Tastes: _____

_____

Comments on Vintage, Region, Winemaker: _____

_____

Recommended   Not Recommended

(Circle One)

WINE: _____ Vintage: _____ Producer: _____

Region/Country: _____ Price: _____ Date Tasted: _____

Grape(s): _____

Importer/Distributor: _____ Alcohol % _____

CIRCLE YOUR RATINGS BELOW.

Color/Style: Red   White   Rosé   Sparkling   Effervescent   Fortified

Appearance: Thin   Translucent   Saturated   Opaque

Dry/Sweet Spectrum: Dry   1   2   3   4   5   6   7   8   9   10   Sweet

Body: Light   Light to Medium   Medium   Medium to Full   Full

Balance: Unbalanced   1   2   3   4   5   6   7   8   9   10   Balanced

Finish: Short   Short to Medium   Medium   Medium to Long   Long

Overall Tasting Experience: Poor   1   2   3   4   5   6   7   8   9   10   Excellent

Price-to-Value Ratio: Poor   1   2   3   4   5   6   7   8   9   10   Excellent

Aromas and Tastes: _____

_____

Comments on Vintage, Region, Winemaker: _____

_____

Recommended	Not Recommended

(Circle One)

WINE: _____ Vintage: _____ Producer: _____

Region/Country: _____ Price: _____ Date Tasted: _____

Grape(s): _____

Importer/Distributor: _____ Alcohol % _____

CIRCLE YOUR RATINGS BELOW.

Color/Style: Red   White   Rosé   Sparkling   Effervescent   Fortified

Appearance: Thin   Translucent   Saturated   Opaque

Dry/Sweet Spectrum: Dry   1   2   3   4   5   6   7   8   9   10   Sweet

Body: Light   Light to Medium   Medium   Medium to Full   Full

Balance: Unbalanced   1   2   3   4   5   6   7   8   9   10   Balanced

Finish: Short   Short to Medium   Medium   Medium to Long   Long

Overall Tasting Experience: Poor   1   2   3   4   5   6   7   8   9   10   Excellent

Price-to-Value Ratio: Poor   1   2   3   4   5   6   7   8   9   10   Excellent

Aromas and Tastes: _____

Comments on Vintage, Region, Winemaker: _____

_____

Recommended   Not Recommended

(Circle One)

38

WINE: _____ Vintage: _____ Producer: _____

Region/Country: _____ Price: _____ Date Tasted: _____

Grape(s): _____

Importer/Distributor: _____ Alcohol % _____

CIRCLE YOUR RATINGS BELOW.

Color/Style: Red   White   Rosé   Sparkling   Effervescent   Fortified

Appearance: Thin   Translucent   Saturated   Opaque

Dry/Sweet Spectrum: Dry   1   2   3   4   5   6   7   8   9   10   Sweet

Body: Light   Light to Medium   Medium   Medium to Full   Full

Balance: Unbalanced   1   2   3   4   5   6   7   8   9   10   Balanced

Finish: Short   Short to Medium   Medium   Medium to Long   Long

Overall Tasting Experience: Poor   1   2   3   4   5   6   7   8   9   10   Excellent

Price-to-Value Ratio: Poor   1   2   3   4   5   6   7   8   9   10   Excellent

Aromas and Tastes: _____

_____

Comments on Vintage, Region, Winemaker: _____

_____

Recommended   Not Recommended

(*Circle One*)

WINE: _____ Vintage: _____ Producer: _____

Region/Country: _____ Price: _____ Date Tasted: _____

Grape(s): _____

Importer/Distributor: _____ Alcohol % _____

CIRCLE YOUR RATINGS BELOW.

Color/Style: Red White Rosé Sparkling Effervescent Fortified

Appearance: Thin Translucent Saturated Opaque

Dry/Sweet Spectrum: Dry 1 2 3 4 5 6 7 8 9 10 Sweet

Body: Light Light to Medium Medium Medium to Full Full

Balance: Unbalanced 1 2 3 4 5 6 7 8 9 10 Balanced

Finish: Short Short to Medium Medium Medium to Long Long

Overall Tasting Experience: Poor 1 2 3 4 5 6 7 8 9 10 Excellent

Price-to-Value Ratio: Poor 1 2 3 4 5 6 7 8 9 10 Excellent

Aromas and Tastes: _____

_____

Comments on Vintage, Region, Winemaker: _____

_____

Recommended		Not Recommended
	(Circle One)	

WINE: _____ Vintage: _____ Producer: _____

Region/Country: _____ Price: _____ Date Tasted: _____

Grape(s): _____

Importer/Distributor: _____ Alcohol % _____

CIRCLE YOUR RATINGS BELOW.

Color/Style: Red White Rosé Sparkling Effervescent Fortified

Appearance: Thin Translucent Saturated Opaque

Dry/Sweet Spectrum: Dry 1 2 3 4 5 6 7 8 9 10 Sweet

Body: Light Light to Medium Medium Medium to Full Full

Balance: Unbalanced 1 2 3 4 5 6 7 8 9 10 Balanced

Finish: Short Short to Medium Medium Medium to Long Long

Overall Tasting Experience: Poor 1 2 3 4 5 6 7 8 9 10 Excellent

Price-to-Value Ratio: Poor 1 2 3 4 5 6 7 8 9 10 Excellent

Aromas and Tastes: ....

....

Comments on Vintage, Region, Winemaker: ....

....

Recommended	Not Recommended

(Circle One)

WINE: _____ Vintage: _____ Producer: _____

Region/Country: _____ Price: _____ Date Tasted: _____

Grape(s): _____

Importer/Distributor: _____ Alcohol % _____

CIRCLE YOUR RATINGS BELOW.

Color/Style: Red White Rosé Sparkling Effervescent Fortified

Appearance: Thin Translucent Saturated Opaque

Dry/Sweet Spectrum: Dry 1 2 3 4 5 6 7 8 9 10 Sweet

Body: Light Light to Medium Medium Medium to Full Full

Balance: Unbalanced 1 2 3 4 5 6 7 8 9 10 Balanced

Finish: Short Short to Medium Medium Medium to Long Long

Overall Tasting Experience: Poor 1 2 3 4 5 6 7 8 9 10 Excellent

Price-to-Value Ratio: Poor 1 2 3 4 5 6 7 8 9 10 Excellent

Aromas and Tastes: _____

_____

Comments on Vintage, Region, Winemaker: _____

_____

Recommended   Not Recommended
             (Circle One)

WINE: _____ Vintage: _____ Producer: _____

Region/Country: _____ Price: _____ Date Tasted: _____

Grape(s): _____

Importer/Distributor: _____ Alcohol % _____

CIRCLE YOUR RATINGS BELOW.

Color/Style: Red White Rosé Sparkling Effervescent Fortified

Appearance: Thin Translucent Saturated Opaque

Dry/Sweet Spectrum: Dry 1 2 3 4 5 6 7 8 9 10 Sweet

Body: Light Light to Medium Medium Medium to Full Full

Balance: Unbalanced 1 2 3 4 5 6 7 8 9 10 Balanced

Finish: Short Short to Medium Medium Medium to Long Long

Overall Tasting Experience: Poor 1 2 3 4 5 6 7 8 9 10 Excellent

Price-to-Value Ratio: Poor 1 2 3 4 5 6 7 8 9 10 Excellent

Aromas and Tastes: _____

_____

Comments on Vintage, Region, Winemaker: _____

_____

Recommended   Not Recommended
              (Circle One)

WINE: _____ Vintage: _____ Producer: _____

Region/Country: _____ Price: _____ Date Tasted: _____

Grape(s): _____

Importer/Distributor: _____ Alcohol % _____

CIRCLE YOUR RATINGS BELOW.

Color/Style: Red White Rosé Sparkling Effervescent Fortified

Appearance: Thin Translucent Saturated Opaque

Dry/Sweet Spectrum: Dry 1 2 3 4 5 6 7 8 9 10 Sweet

Body: Light Light to Medium Medium Medium to Full Full

Balance: Unbalanced 1 2 3 4 5 6 7 8 9 10 Balanced

Finish: Short Short to Medium Medium Medium to Long Long

Overall Tasting Experience: Poor 1 2 3 4 5 6 7 8 9 10 Excellent

Price-to-Value Ratio: Poor 1 2 3 4 5 6 7 8 9 10 Excellent

Aromas and Tastes: _____

Comments on Vintage, Region, Winemaker: _____

Recommended   Not Recommended
                (Circle One)

WINE: _____ Vintage: _____ Producer: _____

Region/Country: _____ Price: _____ Date Tasted: _____

Grape(s): _____

Importer/Distributor: _____ Alcohol % _____

CIRCLE YOUR RATINGS BELOW.

Color/Style: Red   White   Rosé   Sparkling   Effervescent   Fortified

Appearance: Thin   Translucent   Saturated   Opaque

Dry/Sweet Spectrum: Dry   1   2   3   4   5   6   7   8   9   10   Sweet

Body: Light   Light to Medium   Medium   Medium to Full   Full

Balance: Unbalanced   1   2   3   4   5   6   7   8   9   10   Balanced

Finish: Short   Short to Medium   Medium   Medium to Long   Long

Overall Tasting Experience: Poor   1   2   3   4   5   6   7   8   9   10   Excellent

Price-to-Value Ratio: Poor   1   2   3   4   5   6   7   8   9   10   Excellent

Aromas and Tastes: _____

_____

Comments on Vintage, Region, Winemaker: _____

_____

Recommended	Not Recommended

(Circle One)

WINE: _____ Vintage: _____ Producer: _____

Region/Country: _____ Price: _____ Date Tasted: _____

Grape(s): _____

Importer/Distributor: _____ Alcohol % _____

CIRCLE YOUR RATINGS BELOW.

Color/Style: Red   White   Rosé   Sparkling   Effervescent   Fortified

Appearance: Thin   Translucent   Saturated   Opaque

Dry/Sweet Spectrum: Dry   1   2   3   4   5   6   7   8   9   10   Sweet

Body: Light   Light to Medium   Medium   Medium to Full   Full

Balance: Unbalanced   1   2   3   4   5   6   7   8   9   10   Balanced

Finish: Short   Short to Medium   Medium   Medium to Long   Long

Overall Tasting Experience: Poor   1   2   3   4   5   6   7   8   9   10   Excellent

Price-to-Value Ratio: Poor   1   2   3   4   5   6   7   8   9   10   Excellent

Aromas and Tastes: _____

_____

Comments on Vintage, Region, Winemaker: _____

_____

Recommended   Not Recommended
                      (Circle One)

WINE: _____ Vintage: _____ Producer: _____

Region/Country: _____ Price: _____ Date Tasted: _____

Grape(s): _____

Importer/Distributor: _____ Alcohol % _____

CIRCLE YOUR RATINGS BELOW.

Color/Style: Red   White   Rosé   Sparkling   Effervescent   Fortified

Appearance: Thin   Translucent   Saturated   Opaque

Dry/Sweet Spectrum: Dry   1   2   3   4   5   6   7   8   9   10   Sweet

Body: Light   Light to Medium   Medium   Medium to Full   Full

Balance: Unbalanced   1   2   3   4   5   6   7   8   9   10   Balanced

Finish: Short   Short to Medium   Medium   Medium to Long   Long

Overall Tasting Experience: Poor   1   2   3   4   5   6   7   8   9   10   Excellent

Price-to-Value Ratio: Poor   1   2   3   4   5   6   7   8   9   10   Excellent

Aromas and Tastes: _____

_____

Comments on Vintage, Region, Winemaker: _____

_____

Recommended		Not Recommended
	(Circle One)	

WINE: _____ Vintage: _____ Producer: _____

Region/Country: _____ Price: _____ Date Tasted: _____

Grape(s): _____

Importer/Distributor: _____ Alcohol % _____

CIRCLE YOUR RATINGS BELOW.

Color/Style: Red White Rosé Sparkling Effervescent Fortified

Appearance: Thin Translucent Saturated Opaque

Dry/Sweet Spectrum: Dry 1 2 3 4 5 6 7 8 9 10 Sweet

Body: Light Light to Medium Medium Medium to Full Full

Balance: Unbalanced 1 2 3 4 5 6 7 8 9 10 Balanced

Finish: Short Short to Medium Medium Medium to Long Long

Overall Tasting Experience: Poor 1 2 3 4 5 6 7 8 9 10 Excellent

Price-to-Value Ratio: Poor 1 2 3 4 5 6 7 8 9 10 Excellent

Aromas and Tastes: _____

_____

Comments on Vintage, Region, Winemaker: _____

_____

Recommended   Not Recommended
                    (Circle One)

WINE: _____ Vintage: _____ Producer: _____

Region/Country: _____ Price: _____ Date Tasted: _____

Grape(s): _____

Importer/Distributor: _____ Alcohol % _____

CIRCLE YOUR RATINGS BELOW.

Color/Style: Red White Rosé Sparkling Effervescent Fortified

Appearance: Thin Translucent Saturated Opaque

Dry/Sweet Spectrum: Dry 1 2 3 4 5 6 7 8 9 10 Sweet

Body: Light Light to Medium Medium Medium to Full Full

Balance: Unbalanced 1 2 3 4 5 6 7 8 9 10 Balanced

Finish: Short Short to Medium Medium Medium to Long Long

Overall Tasting Experience: Poor 1 2 3 4 5 6 7 8 9 10 Excellent

Price-to-Value Ratio: Poor 1 2 3 4 5 6 7 8 9 10 Excellent

Aromas and Tastes: _____

_____

Comments on Vintage, Region, Winemaker: _____

_____

Recommended	Not Recommended
(Circle One)	

WINE: _____ Vintage: _____ Producer: _____

Region/Country: _____ Price: _____ Date Tasted: _____

Grape(s): _____

Importer/Distributor: _____ Alcohol % _____

CIRCLE YOUR RATINGS BELOW.

Color/Style: Red White Rosé Sparkling Effervescent Fortified

Appearance: Thin Translucent Saturated Opaque

Dry/Sweet Spectrum: Dry 1 2 3 4 5 6 7 8 9 10 Sweet

Body: Light Light to Medium Medium Medium to Full Full

Balance: Unbalanced 1 2 3 4 5 6 7 8 9 10 Balanced

Finish: Short Short to Medium Medium Medium to Long Long

Overall Tasting Experience: Poor 1 2 3 4 5 6 7 8 9 10 Excellent

Price-to-Value Ratio: Poor 1 2 3 4 5 6 7 8 9 10 Excellent

Aromas and Tastes: _____

_____

Comments on Vintage, Region, Winemaker: _____

_____

Recommended   Not Recommended
                   (*Circle One*)

WINE: _____ Vintage: _____ Producer: _____

Region/Country: _____ Price: _____ Date Tasted: _____

Grape(s): _____

Importer/Distributor: _____ Alcohol % _____

CIRCLE YOUR RATINGS BELOW.

Color/Style: Red   White   Rosé   Sparkling   Effervescent   Fortified

Appearance: Thin   Translucent   Saturated   Opaque

Dry/Sweet Spectrum: Dry   1   2   3   4   5   6   7   8   9   10   Sweet

Body: Light   Light to Medium   Medium   Medium to Full   Full

Balance: Unbalanced   1   2   3   4   5   6   7   8   9   10   Balanced

Finish: Short   Short to Medium   Medium   Medium to Long   Long

Overall Tasting Experience: Poor   1   2   3   4   5   6   7   8   9   10   Excellent

Price-to-Value Ratio: Poor   1   2   3   4   5   6   7   8   9   10   Excellent

Aromas and Tastes: _____

_____

Comments on Vintage, Region, Winemaker: _____

_____

Recommended   Not Recommended
                  (*Circle One*)

WINE: _____ Vintage: _____ Producer: _____

Region/Country: _____ Price: _____ Date Tasted: _____

Grape(s): _____

Importer/Distributor: _____ Alcohol % _____

CIRCLE YOUR RATINGS BELOW.

Color/Style: Red White Rosé Sparkling Effervescent Fortified

Appearance: Thin Translucent Saturated Opaque

Dry/Sweet Spectrum: Dry 1 2 3 4 5 6 7 8 9 10 Sweet

Body: Light Light to Medium Medium Medium to Full Full

Balance: Unbalanced 1 2 3 4 5 6 7 8 9 10 Balanced

Finish: Short Short to Medium Medium Medium to Long Long

Overall Tasting Experience: Poor 1 2 3 4 5 6 7 8 9 10 Excellent

Price-to-Value Ratio: Poor 1 2 3 4 5 6 7 8 9 10 Excellent

Aromas and Tastes: _____

_____

Comments on Vintage, Region, Winemaker: _____

_____

Recommended   Not Recommended

(Circle One)

52

WINE: _____ Vintage: _____ Producer: _____

Region/Country: _____ Price: _____ Date Tasted: _____

Grape(s): _____

Importer/Distributor: _____ Alcohol % _____

CIRCLE YOUR RATINGS BELOW.

Color/Style: Red White Rosé Sparkling Effervescent Fortified

Appearance: Thin Translucent Saturated Opaque

Dry/Sweet Spectrum: Dry 1 2 3 4 5 6 7 8 9 10 Sweet

Body: Light Light to Medium Medium Medium to Full Full

Balance: Unbalanced 1 2 3 4 5 6 7 8 9 10 Balanced

Finish: Short Short to Medium Medium Medium to Long Long

Overall Tasting Experience: Poor 1 2 3 4 5 6 7 8 9 10 Excellent

Price-to-Value Ratio: Poor 1 2 3 4 5 6 7 8 9 10 Excellent

Aromas and Tastes: _____

_____

Comments on Vintage, Region, Winemaker: _____

_____

Recommended   Not Recommended
                    (*Circle One*)

WINE: _____ Vintage: _____ Producer: _____

Region/Country: _____ Price: _____ Date Tasted: _____

Grape(s): _____

Importer/Distributor: _____ Alcohol % _____

CIRCLE YOUR RATINGS BELOW.

Color/Style: Red   White   Rosé   Sparkling   Effervescent   Fortified

Appearance: Thin   Translucent   Saturated   Opaque

Dry/Sweet Spectrum: Dry   1   2   3   4   5   6   7   8   9   10   Sweet

Body: Light   Light to Medium   Medium   Medium to Full   Full

Balance: Unbalanced   1   2   3   4   5   6   7   8   9   10   Balanced

Finish: Short   Short to Medium   Medium   Medium to Long   Long

Overall Tasting Experience: Poor   1   2   3   4   5   6   7   8   9   10   Excellent

Price-to-Value Ratio: Poor   1   2   3   4   5   6   7   8   9   10   Excellent

Aromas and Tastes: _____

_____

Comments on Vintage, Region, Winemaker: _____

_____

Recommended	Not Recommended
	(Circle One)	

54

WINE: _____ Vintage: _____ Producer: _____

Region/Country: _____ Price: _____ Date Tasted: _____

Grape(s): _____

Importer/Distributor: _____ Alcohol % _____

CIRCLE YOUR RATINGS BELOW.

Color/Style: Red   White   Rosé   Sparkling   Effervescent   Fortified

Appearance: Thin   Translucent   Saturated   Opaque

Dry/Sweet Spectrum: Dry   1   2   3   4   5   6   7   8   9   10   Sweet

Body: Light   Light to Medium   Medium   Medium to Full   Full

Balance: Unbalanced   1   2   3   4   5   6   7   8   9   10   Balanced

Finish: Short   Short to Medium   Medium   Medium to Long   Long

Overall Tasting Experience: Poor   1   2   3   4   5   6   7   8   9   10   Excellent

Price-to-Value Ratio: Poor   1   2   3   4   5   6   7   8   9   10   Excellent

Aromas and Tastes: _____

_____

Comments on Vintage, Region, Winemaker: _____

_____

Recommended   Not Recommended

(*Circle One*)

WINE: _____ Vintage: _____ Producer: _____

Region/Country: _____ Price: _____ Date Tasted: _____

Grape(s): _____

Importer/Distributor: _____ Alcohol % _____

CIRCLE YOUR RATINGS BELOW.

Color/Style: Red   White   Rosé   Sparkling   Effervescent   Fortified

Appearance: Thin   Translucent   Saturated   Opaque

Dry/Sweet Spectrum: Dry   1   2   3   4   5   6   7   8   9   10   Sweet

Body: Light   Light to Medium   Medium   Medium to Full   Full

Balance: Unbalanced   1   2   3   4   5   6   7   8   9   10   Balanced

Finish: Short   Short to Medium   Medium   Medium to Long   Long

Overall Tasting Experience: Poor   1   2   3   4   5   6   7   8   9   10   Excellent

Price-to-Value Ratio: Poor   1   2   3   4   5   6   7   8   9   10   Excellent

Aromas and Tastes: _____

_____

Comments on Vintage, Region, Winemaker: _____

_____

Recommended		Not Recommended
	(Circle One)	

WINE: _____ Vintage: _____ Producer: _____

Region/Country: _____ Price: _____ Date Tasted: _____

Grape(s): _____

Importer/Distributor: _____ Alcohol % _____

CIRCLE YOUR RATINGS BELOW.

Color/Style: Red White Rosé Sparkling Effervescent Fortified

Appearance: Thin Translucent Saturated Opaque

Dry/Sweet Spectrum: Dry 1 2 3 4 5 6 7 8 9 10 Sweet

Body: Light Light to Medium Medium Medium to Full Full

Balance: Unbalanced 1 2 3 4 5 6 7 8 9 10 Balanced

Finish: Short Short to Medium Medium Medium to Long Long

Overall Tasting Experience: Poor 1 2 3 4 5 6 7 8 9 10 Excellent

Price-to-Value Ratio: Poor 1 2 3 4 5 6 7 8 9 10 Excellent

Aromas and Tastes: _____

_____

Comments on Vintage, Region, Winemaker: _____

_____

Recommended		Not Recommended
	(Circle One)	

WINE: _____ Vintage: _____ Producer: _____

Region/Country: _____ Price: _____ Date Tasted: _____

Grape(s): _____

Importer/Distributor: _____ Alcohol % _____

CIRCLE YOUR RATINGS BELOW.

Color/Style: Red   White   Rosé   Sparkling   Effervescent   Fortified

Appearance: Thin   Translucent   Saturated   Opaque

Dry/Sweet Spectrum: Dry   1   2   3   4   5   6   7   8   9   10   Sweet

Body: Light   Light to Medium   Medium   Medium to Full   Full

Balance: Unbalanced   1   2   3   4   5   6   7   8   9   10   Balanced

Finish: Short   Short to Medium   Medium   Medium to Long   Long

Overall Tasting Experience: Poor   1   2   3   4   5   6   7   8   9   10   Excellent

Price-to-Value Ratio: Poor   1   2   3   4   5   6   7   8   9   10   Excellent

Aromas and Tastes: _____

_____

Comments on Vintage, Region, Winemaker: _____

_____

Recommended	Not Recommended
	(Circle One)	

WINE: _____ Vintage: _____ Producer: _____

Region/Country: _____ Price: _____ Date Tasted: _____

Grape(s): _____

Importer/Distributor: _____ Alcohol % _____

CIRCLE YOUR RATINGS BELOW.

Color/Style: Red White Rosé Sparkling Effervescent Fortified

Appearance: Thin Translucent Saturated Opaque

Dry/Sweet Spectrum: Dry 1 2 3 4 5 6 7 8 9 10 Sweet

Body: Light Light to Medium Medium Medium to Full Full

Balance: Unbalanced 1 2 3 4 5 6 7 8 9 10 Balanced

Finish: Short Short to Medium Medium Medium to Long Long

Overall Tasting Experience: Poor 1 2 3 4 5 6 7 8 9 10 Excellent

Price-to-Value Ratio: Poor 1 2 3 4 5 6 7 8 9 10 Excellent

Aromas and Tastes: _____

_____

Comments on Vintage, Region, Winemaker: _____

_____

Recommended   Not Recommended

(Circle One)

WINE: _____ Vintage: _____ Producer: _____

Region/Country: _____ Price: _____ Date Tasted: _____

Grape(s): _____

Importer/Distributor: _____ Alcohol % _____

CIRCLE YOUR RATINGS BELOW.

Color/Style: Red   White   Rosé   Sparkling   Effervescent   Fortified

Appearance: Thin   Translucent   Saturated   Opaque

Dry/Sweet Spectrum: Dry   1   2   3   4   5   6   7   8   9   10   Sweet

Body: Light   Light to Medium   Medium   Medium to Full   Full

Balance: Unbalanced   1   2   3   4   5   6   7   8   9   10   Balanced

Finish: Short   Short to Medium   Medium   Medium to Long   Long

Overall Tasting Experience: Poor   1   2   3   4   5   6   7   8   9   10   Excellent

Price-to-Value Ratio: Poor   1   2   3   4   5   6   7   8   9   10   Excellent

Aromas and Tastes: _____

_____

Comments on Vintage, Region, Winemaker: _____

_____

Recommended	Not Recommended
	(Circle One)	

WINE: _____ Vintage: _____ Producer: _____

Region/Country: _____ Price: _____ Date Tasted: _____

Grape(s): _____

Importer/Distributor: _____ Alcohol % _____

CIRCLE YOUR RATINGS BELOW.

Color/Style: Red   White   Rosé   Sparkling   Effervescent   Fortified

Appearance: Thin   Translucent   Saturated   Opaque

Dry/Sweet Spectrum: Dry   1   2   3   4   5   6   7   8   9   10   Sweet

Body: Light   Light to Medium   Medium   Medium to Full   Full

Balance: Unbalanced   1   2   3   4   5   6   7   8   9   10   Balanced

Finish: Short   Short to Medium   Medium   Medium to Long   Long

Overall Tasting Experience: Poor   1   2   3   4   5   6   7   8   9   10   Excellent

Price-to-Value Ratio: Poor   1   2   3   4   5   6   7   8   9   10   Excellent

Aromas and Tastes: _____

_____

Comments on Vintage, Region, Winemaker: _____

_____

Recommended	Not Recommended
	(*Circle One*)	

WINE: _____ Vintage: _____ Producer: _____

Region/Country: _____ Price: _____ Date Tasted: _____

Grape(s): _____

Importer/Distributor: _____ Alcohol % _____

CIRCLE YOUR RATINGS BELOW.

Color/Style: Red   White   Rosé   Sparkling   Effervescent   Fortified

Appearance: Thin   Translucent   Saturated   Opaque

Dry/Sweet Spectrum: Dry 1 2 3 4 5 6 7 8 9 10 Sweet

Body: Light   Light to Medium   Medium   Medium to Full   Full

Balance: Unbalanced 1 2 3 4 5 6 7 8 9 10 Balanced

Finish: Short   Short to Medium   Medium   Medium to Long   Long

Overall Tasting Experience: Poor 1 2 3 4 5 6 7 8 9 10 Excellent

Price-to-Value Ratio: Poor 1 2 3 4 5 6 7 8 9 10 Excellent

Aromas and Tastes: _____

_____

Comments on Vintage, Region, Winemaker: _____

_____

Recommended   Not Recommended
                        (Circle One)

WINE: _____ Vintage: _____ Producer: _____

Region/Country: _____ Price: _____ Date Tasted: _____

Grape(s): _____

Importer/Distributor: _____ Alcohol % _____

CIRCLE YOUR RATINGS BELOW.

Color/Style: Red White Rosé Sparkling Effervescent Fortified

Appearance: Thin Translucent Saturated Opaque

Dry/Sweet Spectrum: Dry 1 2 3 4 5 6 7 8 9 10 Sweet

Body: Light Light to Medium Medium Medium to Full Full

Balance: Unbalanced 1 2 3 4 5 6 7 8 9 10 Balanced

Finish: Short Short to Medium Medium Medium to Long Long

Overall Tasting Experience: Poor 1 2 3 4 5 6 7 8 9 10 Excellent

Price-to-Value Ratio: Poor 1 2 3 4 5 6 7 8 9 10 Excellent

Aromas and Tastes: _____

_____

Comments on Vintage, Region, Winemaker: _____

_____

Recommended	Not Recommended
	(Circle One)	

WINE: _____ Vintage: _____ Producer: _____

Region/Country: _____ Price: _____ Date Tasted: _____

Grape(s): _____

Importer/Distributor: _____ Alcohol % _____

CIRCLE YOUR RATINGS BELOW.

Color/Style: Red White Rosé Sparkling Effervescent Fortified

Appearance: Thin Translucent Saturated Opaque

Dry/Sweet Spectrum: Dry 1 2 3 4 5 6 7 8 9 10 Sweet

Body: Light Light to Medium Medium Medium to Full Full

Balance: Unbalanced 1 2 3 4 5 6 7 8 9 10 Balanced

Finish: Short Short to Medium Medium Medium to Long Long

Overall Tasting Experience: Poor 1 2 3 4 5 6 7 8 9 10 Excellent

Price-to-Value Ratio: Poor 1 2 3 4 5 6 7 8 9 10 Excellent

Aromas and Tastes: _____

_____

Comments on Vintage, Region, Winemaker: _____

_____

Recommended   Not Recommended
                (Circle One)

64

WINE: _____ Vintage: _____ Producer: _____

Region/Country: _____ Price: _____ Date Tasted: _____

Grape(s): _____

Importer/Distributor: _____ Alcohol % _____

CIRCLE YOUR RATINGS BELOW.

Color/Style: Red White Rosé Sparkling Effervescent Fortified

Appearance: Thin Translucent Saturated Opaque

Dry/Sweet Spectrum: Dry 1 2 3 4 5 6 7 8 9 10 Sweet

Body: Light Light to Medium Medium Medium to Full Full

Balance: Unbalanced 1 2 3 4 5 6 7 8 9 10 Balanced

Finish: Short Short to Medium Medium Medium to Long Long

Overall Tasting Experience: Poor 1 2 3 4 5 6 7 8 9 10 Excellent

Price-to-Value Ratio: Poor 1 2 3 4 5 6 7 8 9 10 Excellent

Aromas and Tastes: _____

_____

Comments on Vintage, Region, Winemaker: _____

_____

Recommended   Not Recommended

(Circle One)

WINE: _____ Vintage: _____ Producer: _____

Region/Country: _____ Price: _____ Date Tasted: _____

Grape(s): _____

Importer/Distributor: _____ Alcohol % _____

CIRCLE YOUR RATINGS BELOW.

Color/Style: Red   White   Rosé   Sparkling   Effervescent   Fortified

Appearance: Thin   Translucent   Saturated   Opaque

Dry/Sweet Spectrum: Dry   1   2   3   4   5   6   7   8   9   10   Sweet

Body: Light   Light to Medium   Medium   Medium to Full   Full

Balance: Unbalanced   1   2   3   4   5   6   7   8   9   10   Balanced

Finish: Short   Short to Medium   Medium   Medium to Long   Long

Overall Tasting Experience: Poor   1   2   3   4   5   6   7   8   9   10   Excellent

Price-to-Value Ratio: Poor   1   2   3   4   5   6   7   8   9   10   Excellent

Aromas and Tastes: _____

_____

Comments on Vintage, Region, Winemaker: _____

_____

Recommended	Not Recommended

(*Circle One*)

WINE: _____ Vintage: _____ Producer: _____

Region/Country: _____ Price: _____ Date Tasted: _____

Grape(s): _____

Importer/Distributor: _____ Alcohol % _____

CIRCLE YOUR RATINGS BELOW.

Color/Style: Red   White   Rosé   Sparkling   Effervescent   Fortified

Appearance: Thin   Translucent   Saturated   Opaque

Dry/Sweet Spectrum: Dry   1   2   3   4   5   6   7   8   9   10   Sweet

Body: Light   Light to Medium   Medium   Medium to Full   Full

Balance: Unbalanced   1   2   3   4   5   6   7   8   9   10   Balanced

Finish: Short   Short to Medium   Medium   Medium to Long   Long

Overall Tasting Experience: Poor   1   2   3   4   5   6   7   8   9   10   Excellent

Price-to-Value Ratio: Poor   1   2   3   4   5   6   7   8   9   10   Excellent

Aromas and Tastes: _____

_____

Comments on Vintage, Region, Winemaker: _____

_____

Recommended   Not Recommended
                    (*Circle One*)

WINE: _____ Vintage: _____ Producer: _____

Region/Country: _____ Price: _____ Date Tasted: _____

Grape(s): _____

Importer/Distributor: _____ Alcohol % _____

CIRCLE YOUR RATINGS BELOW.

Color/Style: Red White Rosé Sparkling Effervescent Fortified

Appearance: Thin Translucent Saturated Opaque

Dry/Sweet Spectrum: Dry 1 2 3 4 5 6 7 8 9 10 Sweet

Body: Light Light to Medium Medium Medium to Full Full

Balance: Unbalanced 1 2 3 4 5 6 7 8 9 10 Balanced

Finish: Short Short to Medium Medium Medium to Long Long

Overall Tasting Experience: Poor 1 2 3 4 5 6 7 8 9 10 Excellent

Price-to-Value Ratio: Poor 1 2 3 4 5 6 7 8 9 10 Excellent

Aromas and Tastes: _____

_____

Comments on Vintage, Region, Winemaker: _____

_____

Recommended	Not Recommended
	(Circle One)	

68

WINE: _____ Vintage: _____ Producer: _____

Region/Country: _____ Price: _____ Date Tasted: _____

Grape(s): _____

Importer/Distributor: _____ Alcohol % _____

CIRCLE YOUR RATINGS BELOW.

Color/Style: Red   White   Rosé   Sparkling   Effervescent   Fortified

Appearance: Thin   Translucent   Saturated   Opaque

Dry/Sweet Spectrum: Dry   1   2   3   4   5   6   7   8   9   10   Sweet

Body: Light   Light to Medium   Medium   Medium to Full   Full

Balance: Unbalanced   1   2   3   4   5   6   7   8   9   10   Balanced

Finish: Short   Short to Medium   Medium   Medium to Long   Long

Overall Tasting Experience: Poor   1   2   3   4   5   6   7   8   9   10   Excellent

Price-to-Value Ratio: Poor   1   2   3   4   5   6   7   8   9   10   Excellent

Aromas and Tastes: _____

_____

Comments on Vintage, Region, Winemaker: _____

_____

Recommended	Not Recommended
	(Circle One)	

69

WINE: _____ Vintage: _____ Producer: _____

Region/Country: _____ Price: _____ Date Tasted: _____

Grape(s): _____

Importer/Distributor: _____ Alcohol % _____

CIRCLE YOUR RATINGS BELOW.

Color/Style: Red White Rosé Sparkling Effervescent Fortified

Appearance: Thin Translucent Saturated Opaque

Dry/Sweet Spectrum: Dry 1 2 3 4 5 6 7 8 9 10 Sweet

Body: Light Light to Medium Medium Medium to Full Full

Balance: Unbalanced 1 2 3 4 5 6 7 8 9 10 Balanced

Finish: Short Short to Medium Medium Medium to Long Long

Overall Tasting Experience: Poor 1 2 3 4 5 6 7 8 9 10 Excellent

Price-to-Value Ratio: Poor 1 2 3 4 5 6 7 8 9 10 Excellent

Aromas and Tastes: _____

_____

Comments on Vintage, Region, Winemaker: _____

_____

Recommended   Not Recommended

(_Circle One_)

WINE: _____ Vintage: _____ Producer: _____

Region/Country: _____ Price: _____ Date Tasted: _____

Grape(s): _____

Importer/Distributor: _____ Alcohol % _____

CIRCLE YOUR RATINGS BELOW.

Color/Style: Red   White   Rosé   Sparkling   Effervescent   Fortified

Appearance: Thin   Translucent   Saturated   Opaque

Dry/Sweet Spectrum: Dry   1   2   3   4   5   6   7   8   9   10   Sweet

Body: Light   Light to Medium   Medium   Medium to Full   Full

Balance: Unbalanced   1   2   3   4   5   6   7   8   9   10   Balanced

Finish: Short   Short to Medium   Medium   Medium to Long   Long

Overall Tasting Experience: Poor   1   2   3   4   5   6   7   8   9   10   Excellent

Price-to-Value Ratio: Poor   1   2   3   4   5   6   7   8   9   10   Excellent

Aromas and Tastes: _____

_____

Comments on Vintage, Region, Winemaker: _____

_____

Recommended   Not Recommended

(*Circle One*)

WINE: _____ Vintage: _____ Producer: _____

Region/Country: _____ Price: _____ Date Tasted: _____

Grape(s): _____

Importer/Distributor: _____ Alcohol % _____

CIRCLE YOUR RATINGS BELOW.

Color/Style: Red White Rosé Sparkling Effervescent Fortified

Appearance: Thin Translucent Saturated Opaque

Dry/Sweet Spectrum: Dry 1 2 3 4 5 6 7 8 9 10 Sweet

Body: Light Light to Medium Medium Medium to Full Full

Balance: Unbalanced 1 2 3 4 5 6 7 8 9 10 Balanced

Finish: Short Short to Medium Medium Medium to Long Long

Overall Tasting Experience: Poor 1 2 3 4 5 6 7 8 9 10 Excellent

Price-to-Value Ratio: Poor 1 2 3 4 5 6 7 8 9 10 Excellent

Aromas and Tastes: _____

_____

Comments on Vintage, Region, Winemaker: _____

Recommended   Not Recommended
                    (*Circle One*)

72

WINE: _____ Vintage: _____ Producer: _____

Region/Country: _____ Price: _____ Date Tasted: _____

Grape(s): _____

Importer/Distributor: _____ Alcohol % _____

CIRCLE YOUR RATINGS BELOW.

Color/Style: Red   White   Rosé   Sparkling   Effervescent   Fortified

Appearance: Thin   Translucent   Saturated   Opaque

Dry/Sweet Spectrum: Dry   1   2   3   4   5   6   7   8   9   10   Sweet

Body: Light   Light to Medium   Medium   Medium to Full   Full

Balance: Unbalanced   1   2   3   4   5   6   7   8   9   10   Balanced

Finish: Short   Short to Medium   Medium   Medium to Long   Long

Overall Tasting Experience: Poor   1   2   3   4   5   6   7   8   9   10   Excellent

Price-to-Value Ratio: Poor   1   2   3   4   5   6   7   8   9   10   Excellent

Aromas and Tastes: _____

_____

Comments on Vintage, Region, Winemaker: _____

_____

Recommended	Not Recommended

(Circle One)

73

WINE: _____ Vintage: _____ Producer: _____

Region/Country: _____ Price: _____ Date Tasted: _____

Grape(s): _____

Importer/Distributor: _____ Alcohol % _____

CIRCLE YOUR RATINGS BELOW.

Color/Style: Red   White   Rosé   Sparkling   Effervescent   Fortified

Appearance: Thin   Translucent   Saturated   Opaque

Dry/Sweet Spectrum: Dry   1   2   3   4   5   6   7   8   9   10   Sweet

Body: Light   Light to Medium   Medium   Medium to Full   Full

Balance: Unbalanced   1   2   3   4   5   6   7   8   9   10   Balanced

Finish: Short   Short to Medium   Medium   Medium to Long   Long

Overall Tasting Experience: Poor   1   2   3   4   5   6   7   8   9   10   Excellent

Price-to-Value Ratio: Poor   1   2   3   4   5   6   7   8   9   10   Excellent

Aromas and Tastes: _____

_____

Comments on Vintage, Region, Winemaker: _____

_____

Recommended   Not Recommended

(*Circle One*)

WINE: _____ Vintage: _____ Producer: _____

Region/Country: _____ Price: _____ Date Tasted: _____

Grape(s): _____

Importer/Distributor: _____ Alcohol % _____

CIRCLE YOUR RATINGS BELOW.

Color/Style: Red White Rosé Sparkling Effervescent Fortified

Appearance: Thin Translucent Saturated Opaque

Dry/Sweet Spectrum: Dry 1 2 3 4 5 6 7 8 9 10 Sweet

Body: Light Light to Medium Medium Medium to Full Full

Balance: Unbalanced 1 2 3 4 5 6 7 8 9 10 Balanced

Finish: Short Short to Medium Medium Medium to Long Long

Overall Tasting Experience: Poor 1 2 3 4 5 6 7 8 9 10 Excellent

Price-to-Value Ratio: Poor 1 2 3 4 5 6 7 8 9 10 Excellent

Aromas and Tastes: _____

_____

Comments on Vintage, Region, Winemaker: _____

_____

Recommended   Not Recommended
                    (Circle One)

75

WINE: _____ Vintage: _____ Producer: _____

Region/Country: _____ Price: _____ Date Tasted: _____

Grape(s): _____

Importer/Distributor: _____ Alcohol % _____

CIRCLE YOUR RATINGS BELOW.

Color/Style: Red White Rosé Sparkling Effervescent Fortified

Appearance: Thin Translucent Saturated Opaque

Dry/Sweet Spectrum: Dry 1 2 3 4 5 6 7 8 9 10 Sweet

Body: Light Light to Medium Medium Medium to Full Full

Balance: Unbalanced 1 2 3 4 5 6 7 8 9 10 Balanced

Finish: Short Short to Medium Medium Medium to Long Long

Overall Tasting Experience: Poor 1 2 3 4 5 6 7 8 9 10 Excellent

Price-to-Value Ratio: Poor 1 2 3 4 5 6 7 8 9 10 Excellent

Aromas and Tastes: _____

_____

Comments on Vintage, Region, Winemaker: _____

_____

Recommended   Not Recommended

(*Circle One*)

WINE: _____ Vintage: _____ Producer: _____

Region/Country: _____ Price: _____ Date Tasted: _____

Grape(s): _____

Importer/Distributor: _____ Alcohol % _____

CIRCLE YOUR RATINGS BELOW.

Color/Style: Red   White   Rosé   Sparkling   Effervescent   Fortified

Appearance: Thin   Translucent   Saturated   Opaque

Dry/Sweet Spectrum: Dry   1   2   3   4   5   6   7   8   9   10   Sweet

Body: Light   Light to Medium   Medium   Medium to Full   Full

Balance: Unbalanced   1   2   3   4   5   6   7   8   9   10   Balanced

Finish: Short   Short to Medium   Medium   Medium to Long   Long

Overall Tasting Experience: Poor   1   2   3   4   5   6   7   8   9   10   Excellent

Price-to-Value Ratio: Poor   1   2   3   4   5   6   7   8   9   10   Excellent

Aromas and Tastes: _____

_____

Comments on Vintage, Region, Winemaker: _____

_____

Recommended	Not Recommended
	(Circle One)	

WINE: _____ Vintage: _____ Producer: _____

Region/Country: _____ Price: _____ Date Tasted: _____

Grape(s): _____

Importer/Distributor: _____ Alcohol % _____

CIRCLE YOUR RATINGS BELOW.

Color/Style: Red White Rosé Sparkling Effervescent Fortified

Appearance: Thin Translucent Saturated Opaque

Dry/Sweet Spectrum: Dry 1 2 3 4 5 6 7 8 9 10 Sweet

Body: Light Light to Medium Medium Medium to Full Full

Balance: Unbalanced 1 2 3 4 5 6 7 8 9 10 Balanced

Finish: Short Short to Medium Medium Medium to Long Long

Overall Tasting Experience: Poor 1 2 3 4 5 6 7 8 9 10 Excellent

Price-to-Value Ratio: Poor 1 2 3 4 5 6 7 8 9 10 Excellent

Aromas and Tastes: _____

_____

Comments on Vintage, Region, Winemaker: _____

_____

Recommended   Not Recommended
                    (*Circle One*)

WINE: _____ Vintage: _____ Producer: _____

Region/Country: _____ Price: _____ Date Tasted: _____

Grape(s): _____

Importer/Distributor: _____ Alcohol % _____

CIRCLE YOUR RATINGS BELOW.

Color/Style: Red   White   Rosé   Sparkling   Effervescent   Fortified

Appearance: Thin   Translucent   Saturated   Opaque

Dry/Sweet Spectrum: Dry   1   2   3   4   5   6   7   8   9   10   Sweet

Body: Light   Light to Medium   Medium   Medium to Full   Full

Balance: Unbalanced   1   2   3   4   5   6   7   8   9   10   Balanced

Finish: Short   Short to Medium   Medium   Medium to Long   Long

Overall Tasting Experience: Poor   1   2   3   4   5   6   7   8   9   10   Excellent

Price-to-Value Ratio: Poor   1   2   3   4   5   6   7   8   9   10   Excellent

Aromas and Tastes: _____

_____

Comments on Vintage, Region, Winemaker: _____

_____

Recommended	Not Recommended
	(*Circle One*)

WINE: _____ Vintage: _____ Producer: _____

Region/Country: _____ Price: _____ Date Tasted: _____

Grape(s): _____

Importer/Distributor: _____ Alcohol % _____

CIRCLE YOUR RATINGS BELOW.

Color/Style: Red White Rosé Sparkling Effervescent Fortified

Appearance: Thin Translucent Saturated Opaque

Dry/Sweet Spectrum: Dry 1 2 3 4 5 6 7 8 9 10 Sweet

Body: Light Light to Medium Medium Medium to Full Full

Balance: Unbalanced 1 2 3 4 5 6 7 8 9 10 Balanced

Finish: Short Short to Medium Medium Medium to Long Long

Overall Tasting Experience: Poor 1 2 3 4 5 6 7 8 9 10 Excellent

Price-to-Value Ratio: Poor 1 2 3 4 5 6 7 8 9 10 Excellent

Aromas and Tastes: _____

_____

Comments on Vintage, Region, Winemaker: _____

_____

Recommended   Not Recommended

(Circle One)

80

WINE: _____ Vintage: _____ Producer: _____

Region/Country: _____ Price: _____ Date Tasted: _____

Grape(s): _____

Importer/Distributor: _____ Alcohol % _____

CIRCLE YOUR RATINGS BELOW.

Color/Style: Red   White   Rosé   Sparkling   Effervescent   Fortified

Appearance: Thin   Translucent   Saturated   Opaque

Dry/Sweet Spectrum: Dry   1   2   3   4   5   6   7   8   9   10   Sweet

Body: Light   Light to Medium   Medium   Medium to Full   Full

Balance: Unbalanced   1   2   3   4   5   6   7   8   9   10   Balanced

Finish: Short   Short to Medium   Medium   Medium to Long   Long

Overall Tasting Experience: Poor   1   2   3   4   5   6   7   8   9   10   Excellent

Price-to-Value Ratio: Poor   1   2   3   4   5   6   7   8   9   10   Excellent

Aromas and Tastes: _____

_____

Comments on Vintage, Region, Winemaker: _____

_____

Recommended		Not Recommended
	(Circle One)	

WINE: _____ Vintage: _____ Producer: _____

Region/Country: _____ Price: _____ Date Tasted: _____

Grape(s): _____

Importer/Distributor: _____ Alcohol % _____

CIRCLE YOUR RATINGS BELOW.

Color/Style: Red White Rosé Sparkling Effervescent Fortified

Appearance: Thin Translucent Saturated Opaque

Dry/Sweet Spectrum: Dry 1 2 3 4 5 6 7 8 9 10 Sweet

Body: Light Light to Medium Medium Medium to Full Full

Balance: Unbalanced 1 2 3 4 5 6 7 8 9 10 Balanced

Finish: Short Short to Medium Medium Medium to Long Long

Overall Tasting Experience: Poor 1 2 3 4 5 6 7 8 9 10 Excellent

Price-to-Value Ratio: Poor 1 2 3 4 5 6 7 8 9 10 Excellent

Aromas and Tastes: _____

_____

Comments on Vintage, Region, Winemaker: _____

_____

Recommended	Not Recommended
	(Circle One)

WINE: _____ Vintage: _____ Producer: _____

Region/Country: _____ Price: _____ Date Tasted: _____

Grape(s): _____

Importer/Distributor: _____ Alcohol % _____

CIRCLE YOUR RATINGS BELOW.

Color/Style: Red White Rosé Sparkling Effervescent Fortified

Appearance: Thin Translucent Saturated Opaque

Dry/Sweet Spectrum: Dry 1 2 3 4 5 6 7 8 9 10 Sweet

Body: Light Light to Medium Medium Medium to Full Full

Balance: Unbalanced 1 2 3 4 5 6 7 8 9 10 Balanced

Finish: Short Short to Medium Medium Medium to Long Long

Overall Tasting Experience: Poor 1 2 3 4 5 6 7 8 9 10 Excellent

Price-to-Value Ratio: Poor 1 2 3 4 5 6 7 8 9 10 Excellent

Aromas and Tastes: _____

_____

Comments on Vintage, Region, Winemaker: _____

_____

Recommended		Not Recommended
	(*Circle One*)	

WINE: _____ Vintage: _____ Producer: _____

Region/Country: _____ Price: _____ Date Tasted: _____

Grape(s): _____

Importer/Distributor: _____ Alcohol % _____

CIRCLE YOUR RATINGS BELOW.

Color/Style: Red White Rosé Sparkling Effervescent Fortified

Appearance: Thin Translucent Saturated Opaque

Dry/Sweet Spectrum: Dry 1 2 3 4 5 6 7 8 9 10 Sweet

Body: Light Light to Medium Medium Medium to Full Full

Balance: Unbalanced 1 2 3 4 5 6 7 8 9 10 Balanced

Finish: Short Short to Medium Medium Medium to Long Long

Overall Tasting Experience: Poor 1 2 3 4 5 6 7 8 9 10 Excellent

Price-to-Value Ratio: Poor 1 2 3 4 5 6 7 8 9 10 Excellent

Aromas and Tastes: _____

_____

Comments on Vintage, Region, Winemaker: _____

_____

Recommended   Not Recommended
                    (*Circle One*)

WINE: _____ Vintage: _____ Producer: _____

Region/Country: _____ Price: _____ Date Tasted: _____

Grape(s): _____

Importer/Distributor: _____ Alcohol % _____

CIRCLE YOUR RATINGS BELOW.

Color/Style: Red   White   Rosé   Sparkling   Effervescent   Fortified

Appearance: Thin   Translucent   Saturated   Opaque

Dry/Sweet Spectrum: Dry   1   2   3   4   5   6   7   8   9   10   Sweet

Body: Light   Light to Medium   Medium   Medium to Full   Full

Balance: Unbalanced   1   2   3   4   5   6   7   8   9   10   Balanced

Finish: Short   Short to Medium   Medium   Medium to Long   Long

Overall Tasting Experience: Poor   1   2   3   4   5   6   7   8   9   10   Excellent

Price-to-Value Ratio: Poor   1   2   3   4   5   6   7   8   9   10   Excellent

Aromas and Tastes: _____

_____

Comments on Vintage, Region, Winemaker: _____

_____

Recommended		Not Recommended
	(Circle One)	

WINE: _____ Vintage: _____ Producer: _____

Region/Country: _____ Price: _____ Date Tasted: _____

Grape(s): _____

Importer/Distributor: _____ Alcohol % _____

CIRCLE YOUR RATINGS BELOW.

Color/Style: Red White Rosé Sparkling Effervescent Fortified

Appearance: Thin Translucent Saturated Opaque

Dry/Sweet Spectrum: Dry 1 2 3 4 5 6 7 8 9 10 Sweet

Body: Light Light to Medium Medium Medium to Full Full

Balance: Unbalanced 1 2 3 4 5 6 7 8 9 10 Balanced

Finish: Short Short to Medium Medium Medium to Long Long

Overall Tasting Experience: Poor 1 2 3 4 5 6 7 8 9 10 Excellent

Price-to-Value Ratio: Poor 1 2 3 4 5 6 7 8 9 10 Excellent

Aromas and Tastes: _____

_____

Comments on Vintage, Region, Winemaker: _____

_____

Recommended	Not Recommended
	(*Circle One*)

WINE: _____ Vintage: _____ Producer: _____

Region/Country: _____ Price: _____ Date Tasted: _____

Grape(s): _____

Importer/Distributor: _____ Alcohol % _____

CIRCLE YOUR RATINGS BELOW.

Color/Style: Red   White   Rosé   Sparkling   Effervescent   Fortified

Appearance: Thin   Translucent   Saturated   Opaque

Dry/Sweet Spectrum: Dry   1   2   3   4   5   6   7   8   9   10   Sweet

Body: Light   Light to Medium   Medium   Medium to Full   Full

Balance: Unbalanced   1   2   3   4   5   6   7   8   9   10   Balanced

Finish: Short   Short to Medium   Medium   Medium to Long   Long

Overall Tasting Experience: Poor   1   2   3   4   5   6   7   8   9   10   Excellent

Price-to-Value Ratio: Poor   1   2   3   4   5   6   7   8   9   10   Excellent

Aromas and Tastes: _____

_____

Comments on Vintage, Region, Winemaker: _____

_____

Recommended   Not Recommended

(Circle One)

WINE: _____ Vintage: _____ Producer: _____

Region/Country: _____ Price: _____ Date Tasted: _____

Grape(s): _____

Importer/Distributor: _____ Alcohol % _____

CIRCLE YOUR RATINGS BELOW.

Color/Style: Red White Rosé Sparkling Effervescent Fortified

Appearance: Thin Translucent Saturated Opaque

Dry/Sweet Spectrum: Dry 1 2 3 4 5 6 7 8 9 10 Sweet

Body: Light Light to Medium Medium Medium to Full Full

Balance: Unbalanced 1 2 3 4 5 6 7 8 9 10 Balanced

Finish: Short Short to Medium Medium Medium to Long Long

Overall Tasting Experience: Poor 1 2 3 4 5 6 7 8 9 10 Excellent

Price-to-Value Ratio: Poor 1 2 3 4 5 6 7 8 9 10 Excellent

Aromas and Tastes: _____

_____

Comments on Vintage, Region, Winemaker: _____

_____

Recommended		Not Recommended
	(Circle One)	

WINE: _____ Vintage: _____ Producer: _____

Region/Country: _____ Price: _____ Date Tasted: _____

Grape(s): _____

Importer/Distributor: _____ Alcohol % _____

CIRCLE YOUR RATINGS BELOW.

Color/Style: Red White Rosé Sparkling Effervescent Fortified

Appearance: Thin Translucent Saturated Opaque

Dry/Sweet Spectrum: Dry 1 2 3 4 5 6 7 8 9 10 Sweet

Body: Light Light to Medium Medium Medium to Full Full

Balance: Unbalanced 1 2 3 4 5 6 7 8 9 10 Balanced

Finish: Short Short to Medium Medium Medium to Long Long

Overall Tasting Experience: Poor 1 2 3 4 5 6 7 8 9 10 Excellent

Price-to-Value Ratio: Poor 1 2 3 4 5 6 7 8 9 10 Excellent

Aromas and Tastes: _____

_____

Comments on Vintage, Region, Winemaker: _____

_____

Recommended   Not Recommended

(Circle One)

WINE: _____ Vintage: _____ Producer: _____

Region/Country: _____ Price: _____ Date Tasted: _____

Grape(s): _____

Importer/Distributor: _____ Alcohol % _____

CIRCLE YOUR RATINGS BELOW.

Color/Style: Red White Rosé Sparkling Effervescent Fortified

Appearance: Thin Translucent Saturated Opaque

Dry/Sweet Spectrum: Dry 1 2 3 4 5 6 7 8 9 10 Sweet

Body: Light Light to Medium Medium Medium to Full Full

Balance: Unbalanced 1 2 3 4 5 6 7 8 9 10 Balanced

Finish: Short Short to Medium Medium Medium to Long Long

Overall Tasting Experience: Poor 1 2 3 4 5 6 7 8 9 10 Excellent

Price-to-Value Ratio: Poor 1 2 3 4 5 6 7 8 9 10 Excellent

Aromas and Tastes: _____

_____

Comments on Vintage, Region, Winemaker: _____

_____

Recommended   Not Recommended
                    (Circle One)

WINE: _____ Vintage: _____ Producer: _____

Region/Country: _____ Price: _____ Date Tasted: _____

Grape(s): _____

Importer/Distributor: _____ Alcohol % _____

CIRCLE YOUR RATINGS BELOW.

Color/Style: Red   White   Rosé   Sparkling   Effervescent   Fortified

Appearance: Thin   Translucent   Saturated   Opaque

Dry/Sweet Spectrum: Dry   1   2   3   4   5   6   7   8   9   10   Sweet

Body: Light   Light to Medium   Medium   Medium to Full   Full

Balance: Unbalanced   1   2   3   4   5   6   7   8   9   10   Balanced

Finish: Short   Short to Medium   Medium   Medium to Long   Long

Overall Tasting Experience: Poor   1   2   3   4   5   6   7   8   9   10   Excellent

Price-to-Value Ratio: Poor   1   2   3   4   5   6   7   8   9   10   Excellent

Aromas and Tastes: _____

_____

Comments on Vintage, Region, Winemaker: _____

_____

Recommended   Not Recommended
            (*Circle One*)

WINE: _____ Vintage: _____ Producer: _____

Region/Country: _____ Price: _____ Date Tasted: _____

Grape(s): _____

Importer/Distributor: _____ Alcohol % _____

CIRCLE YOUR RATINGS BELOW.

Color/Style: Red White Rosé Sparkling Effervescent Fortified

Appearance: Thin Translucent Saturated Opaque

Dry/Sweet Spectrum: Dry 1 2 3 4 5 6 7 8 9 10 Sweet

Body: Light Light to Medium Medium Medium to Full Full

Balance: Unbalanced 1 2 3 4 5 6 7 8 9 10 Balanced

Finish: Short Short to Medium Medium Medium to Long Long

Overall Tasting Experience: Poor 1 2 3 4 5 6 7 8 9 10 Excellent

Price-to-Value Ratio: Poor 1 2 3 4 5 6 7 8 9 10 Excellent

Aromas and Tastes: _____

_____

Comments on Vintage, Region, Winemaker: _____

_____

Recommended	Not Recommended
(Circle One)	

WINE: _____ Vintage: _____ Producer: _____

Region/Country: _____ Price: _____ Date Tasted: _____

Grape(s): _____

Importer/Distributor: _____ Alcohol % _____

CIRCLE YOUR RATINGS BELOW.

Color/Style: Red White Rosé Sparkling Effervescent Fortified

Appearance: Thin Translucent Saturated Opaque

Dry/Sweet Spectrum: Dry 1 2 3 4 5 6 7 8 9 10 Sweet

Body: Light Light to Medium Medium Medium to Full Full

Balance: Unbalanced 1 2 3 4 5 6 7 8 9 10 Balanced

Finish: Short Short to Medium Medium Medium to Long Long

Overall Tasting Experience: Poor 1 2 3 4 5 6 7 8 9 10 Excellent

Price-to-Value Ratio: Poor 1 2 3 4 5 6 7 8 9 10 Excellent

Aromas and Tastes: _____

_____

Comments on Vintage, Region, Winemaker: _____

_____

Recommended		Not Recommended
	(*Circle One*)	

WINE: _____ Vintage: _____ Producer: _____

Region/Country: _____ Price: _____ Date Tasted: _____

Grape(s): _____

Importer/Distributor: _____ Alcohol % _____

CIRCLE YOUR RATINGS BELOW.

Color/Style: Red White Rosé Sparkling Effervescent Fortified

Appearance: Thin Translucent Saturated Opaque

Dry/Sweet Spectrum: Dry 1 2 3 4 5 6 7 8 9 10 Sweet

Body: Light Light to Medium Medium Medium to Full Full

Balance: Unbalanced 1 2 3 4 5 6 7 8 9 10 Balanced

Finish: Short Short to Medium Medium Medium to Long Long

Overall Tasting Experience: Poor 1 2 3 4 5 6 7 8 9 10 Excellent

Price-to-Value Ratio: Poor 1 2 3 4 5 6 7 8 9 10 Excellent

Aromas and Tastes: _____

Comments on Vintage, Region, Winemaker: _____
_____

Recommended   Not Recommended
                    (*Circle One*)

WINE: _____ Vintage: _____ Producer: _____

Region/Country: _____ Price: _____ Date Tasted: _____

Grape(s): _____

Importer/Distributor: _____ Alcohol % _____

CIRCLE YOUR RATINGS BELOW.

Color/Style: Red White Rosé Sparkling Effervescent Fortified

Appearance: Thin Translucent Saturated Opaque

Dry/Sweet Spectrum: Dry 1 2 3 4 5 6 7 8 9 10 Sweet

Body: Light Light to Medium Medium Medium to Full Full

Balance: Unbalanced 1 2 3 4 5 6 7 8 9 10 Balanced

Finish: Short Short to Medium Medium Medium to Long Long

Overall Tasting Experience: Poor 1 2 3 4 5 6 7 8 9 10 Excellent

Price-to-Value Ratio: Poor 1 2 3 4 5 6 7 8 9 10 Excellent

Aromas and Tastes: _____

_____

Comments on Vintage, Region, Winemaker: _____

_____

Recommended	Not Recommended

(Circle One)

WINE: _____ Vintage: _____ Producer: _____

Region/Country: _____ Price: _____ Date Tasted: _____

Grape(s): _____

Importer/Distributor: _____ Alcohol % _____

CIRCLE YOUR RATINGS BELOW.

Color/Style: Red   White   Rosé   Sparkling   Effervescent   Fortified

Appearance: Thin   Translucent   Saturated   Opaque

Dry/Sweet Spectrum: Dry   1   2   3   4   5   6   7   8   9   10   Sweet

Body: Light   Light to Medium   Medium   Medium to Full   Full

Balance: Unbalanced   1   2   3   4   5   6   7   8   9   10   Balanced

Finish: Short   Short to Medium   Medium   Medium to Long   Long

Overall Tasting Experience: Poor   1   2   3   4   5   6   7   8   9   10   Excellent

Price-to-Value Ratio: Poor   1   2   3   4   5   6   7   8   9   10   Excellent

Aromas and Tastes: _____

_____

Comments on Vintage, Region, Winemaker: _____

_____

Recommended	Not Recommended
	(Circle One)	

WINE: _____ Vintage: _____ Producer: _____

Region/Country: _____ Price: _____ Date Tasted: _____

Grape(s): _____

Importer/Distributor: _____ Alcohol % _____

CIRCLE YOUR RATINGS BELOW.

Color/Style: Red   White   Rosé   Sparkling   Effervescent   Fortified

Appearance: Thin   Translucent   Saturated   Opaque

Dry/Sweet Spectrum: Dry   1   2   3   4   5   6   7   8   9   10   Sweet

Body: Light   Light to Medium   Medium   Medium to Full   Full

Balance: Unbalanced   1   2   3   4   5   6   7   8   9   10   Balanced

Finish: Short   Short to Medium   Medium   Medium to Long   Long

Overall Tasting Experience: Poor   1   2   3   4   5   6   7   8   9   10   Excellent

Price-to-Value Ratio: Poor   1   2   3   4   5   6   7   8   9   10   Excellent

Aromas and Tastes: _____

_____

Comments on Vintage, Region, Winemaker: _____

_____

Recommended   Not Recommended

(Circle One)

WINE: _____ Vintage: _____ Producer: _____

Region/Country: _____ Price: _____ Date Tasted: _____

Grape(s): _____

Importer/Distributor: _____ Alcohol % _____

CIRCLE YOUR RATINGS BELOW.

Color/Style: Red White Rosé Sparkling Effervescent Fortified

Appearance: Thin Translucent Saturated Opaque

Dry/Sweet Spectrum: Dry 1 2 3 4 5 6 7 8 9 10 Sweet

Body: Light Light to Medium Medium Medium to Full Full

Balance: Unbalanced 1 2 3 4 5 6 7 8 9 10 Balanced

Finish: Short Short to Medium Medium Medium to Long Long

Overall Tasting Experience: Poor 1 2 3 4 5 6 7 8 9 10 Excellent

Price-to-Value Ratio: Poor 1 2 3 4 5 6 7 8 9 10 Excellent

Aromas and Tastes: _____

_____

Comments on Vintage, Region, Winemaker: _____

_____

Recommended	Not Recommended

(*Circle One*)

WINE: _____ Vintage: _____ Producer: _____

Region/Country: _____ Price: _____ Date Tasted: _____

Grape(s): _____

Importer/Distributor: _____ Alcohol % _____

CIRCLE YOUR RATINGS BELOW.

Color/Style: Red   White   Rosé   Sparkling   Effervescent   Fortified

Appearance: Thin   Translucent   Saturated   Opaque

Dry/Sweet Spectrum: Dry   1   2   3   4   5   6   7   8   9   10   Sweet

Body: Light   Light to Medium   Medium   Medium to Full   Full

Balance: Unbalanced   1   2   3   4   5   6   7   8   9   10   Balanced

Finish: Short   Short to Medium   Medium   Medium to Long   Long

Overall Tasting Experience: Poor   1   2   3   4   5   6   7   8   9   10   Excellent

Price-to-Value Ratio: Poor   1   2   3   4   5   6   7   8   9   10   Excellent

Aromas and Tastes: _____

_____

Comments on Vintage, Region, Winemaker: _____

_____

Recommended		Not Recommended
	(Circle One)	

WINE: _____ Vintage: _____ Producer: _____

Region/Country: _____ Price: _____ Date Tasted: _____

Grape(s): _____

Importer/Distributor: _____ Alcohol % _____

CIRCLE YOUR RATINGS BELOW.

Color/Style: Red   White   Rosé   Sparkling   Effervescent   Fortified

Appearance: Thin   Translucent   Saturated   Opaque

Dry/Sweet Spectrum: Dry   1   2   3   4   5   6   7   8   9   10   Sweet

Body: Light   Light to Medium   Medium   Medium to Full   Full

Balance: Unbalanced   1   2   3   4   5   6   7   8   9   10   Balanced

Finish: Short   Short to Medium   Medium   Medium to Long   Long

Overall Tasting Experience: Poor   1   2   3   4   5   6   7   8   9   10   Excellent

Price-to-Value Ratio: Poor   1   2   3   4   5   6   7   8   9   10   Excellent

Aromas and Tastes: _____

_____

Comments on Vintage, Region, Winemaker: _____

_____

Recommended   Not Recommended

(Circle One)

WINE: _____ Vintage: _____ Producer: _____

Region/Country: _____ Price: _____ Date Tasted: _____

Grape(s): _____

Importer/Distributor: _____ Alcohol % _____

CIRCLE YOUR RATINGS BELOW.

Color/Style: Red White Rosé Sparkling Effervescent Fortified

Appearance: Thin Translucent Saturated Opaque

Dry/Sweet Spectrum: Dry 1 2 3 4 5 6 7 8 9 10 Sweet

Body: Light Light to Medium Medium Medium to Full Full

Balance: Unbalanced 1 2 3 4 5 6 7 8 9 10 Balanced

Finish: Short Short to Medium Medium Medium to Long Long

Overall Tasting Experience: Poor 1 2 3 4 5 6 7 8 9 10 Excellent

Price-to-Value Ratio: Poor 1 2 3 4 5 6 7 8 9 10 Excellent

Aromas and Tastes: _____

_____

Comments on Vintage, Region, Winemaker: _____

_____

Recommended		Not Recommended
	(Circle One)	

WINE: _____ Vintage: _____ Producer: _____

Region/Country: _____ Price: _____ Date Tasted: _____

Grape(s): _____

Importer/Distributor: _____ Alcohol % _____

CIRCLE YOUR RATINGS BELOW.

Color/Style: Red White Rosé Sparkling Effervescent Fortified

Appearance: Thin Translucent Saturated Opaque

Dry/Sweet Spectrum: Dry 1 2 3 4 5 6 7 8 9 10 Sweet

Body: Light Light to Medium Medium Medium to Full Full

Balance: Unbalanced 1 2 3 4 5 6 7 8 9 10 Balanced

Finish: Short Short to Medium Medium Medium to Long Long

Overall Tasting Experience: Poor 1 2 3 4 5 6 7 8 9 10 Excellent

Price-to-Value Ratio: Poor 1 2 3 4 5 6 7 8 9 10 Excellent

Aromas and Tastes: _____

_____

Comments on Vintage, Region, Winemaker: _____

_____

Recommended   Not Recommended

(*Circle One*)

WINE: _____ Vintage: _____ Producer: _____

Region/Country: _____ Price: _____ Date Tasted: _____

Grape(s): _____

Importer/Distributor: _____ Alcohol % _____

CIRCLE YOUR RATINGS BELOW.

Color/Style: Red White Rosé Sparkling Effervescent Fortified

Appearance: Thin Translucent Saturated Opaque

Dry/Sweet Spectrum: Dry 1 2 3 4 5 6 7 8 9 10 Sweet

Body: Light Light to Medium Medium Medium to Full Full

Balance: Unbalanced 1 2 3 4 5 6 7 8 9 10 Balanced

Finish: Short Short to Medium Medium Medium to Long Long

Overall Tasting Experience: Poor 1 2 3 4 5 6 7 8 9 10 Excellent

Price-to-Value Ratio: Poor 1 2 3 4 5 6 7 8 9 10 Excellent

Aromas and Tastes: _____

_____

Comments on Vintage, Region, Winemaker: _____

_____

Recommended	Not Recommended

(*Circle One*)

WINE: _____ Vintage: _____ Producer: _____

Region/Country: _____ Price: _____ Date Tasted: _____

Grape(s): _____

Importer/Distributor: _____ Alcohol % _____

CIRCLE YOUR RATINGS BELOW.

Color/Style: Red White Rosé Sparkling Effervescent Fortified

Appearance: Thin Translucent Saturated Opaque

Dry/Sweet Spectrum: Dry 1 2 3 4 5 6 7 8 9 10 Sweet

Body: Light Light to Medium Medium Medium to Full Full

Balance: Unbalanced 1 2 3 4 5 6 7 8 9 10 Balanced

Finish: Short Short to Medium Medium Medium to Long Long

Overall Tasting Experience: Poor 1 2 3 4 5 6 7 8 9 10 Excellent

Price-to-Value Ratio: Poor 1 2 3 4 5 6 7 8 9 10 Excellent

Aromas and Tastes: _____

_____

Comments on Vintage, Region, Winemaker: _____

_____

Recommended   Not Recommended
                 (Circle One)

WINE: _____ Vintage: _____ Producer: _____

Region/Country: _____ Price: _____ Date Tasted: _____

Grape(s): _____

Importer/Distributor: _____ Alcohol % _____

CIRCLE YOUR RATINGS BELOW.

Color/Style: Red White Rosé Sparkling Effervescent Fortified

Appearance: Thin Translucent Saturated Opaque

Dry/Sweet Spectrum: Dry 1 2 3 4 5 6 7 8 9 10 Sweet

Body: Light Light to Medium Medium Medium to Full Full

Balance: Unbalanced 1 2 3 4 5 6 7 8 9 10 Balanced

Finish: Short Short to Medium Medium Medium to Long Long

Overall Tasting Experience: Poor 1 2 3 4 5 6 7 8 9 10 Excellent

Price-to-Value Ratio: Poor 1 2 3 4 5 6 7 8 9 10 Excellent

Aromas and Tastes: _____

_____

Comments on Vintage, Region, Winemaker: _____

_____

Recommended	Not Recommended
(Circle One)	

WINE: _____ Vintage: _____ Producer: _____

Region/Country: _____ Price: _____ Date Tasted: _____

Grape(s): _____

Importer/Distributor: _____ Alcohol % _____

CIRCLE YOUR RATINGS BELOW.

Color/Style: Red   White   Rosé   Sparkling   Effervescent   Fortified

Appearance: Thin   Translucent   Saturated   Opaque

Dry/Sweet Spectrum: Dry   1   2   3   4   5   6   7   8   9   10   Sweet

Body: Light   Light to Medium   Medium   Medium to Full   Full

Balance: Unbalanced   1   2   3   4   5   6   7   8   9   10   Balanced

Finish: Short   Short to Medium   Medium   Medium to Long   Long

Overall Tasting Experience: Poor   1   2   3   4   5   6   7   8   9   10   Excellent

Price-to-Value Ratio: Poor   1   2   3   4   5   6   7   8   9   10   Excellent

Aromas and Tastes: _____

_____

_____

Comments on Vintage, Region, Winemaker: _____

_____

Recommended	Not Recommended
	(Circle One)	

WINE: _____ Vintage: _____ Producer: _____

Region/Country: _____ Price: _____ Date Tasted: _____

Grape(s): _____

Importer/Distributor: _____ Alcohol % _____

CIRCLE YOUR RATINGS BELOW.

Color/Style: Red   White   Rosé   Sparkling   Effervescent   Fortified

Appearance: Thin   Translucent   Saturated   Opaque

Dry/Sweet Spectrum: Dry   1   2   3   4   5   6   7   8   9   10   Sweet

Body: Light   Light to Medium   Medium   Medium to Full   Full

Balance: Unbalanced   1   2   3   4   5   6   7   8   9   10   Balanced

Finish: Short   Short to Medium   Medium   Medium to Long   Long

Overall Tasting Experience: Poor   1   2   3   4   5   6   7   8   9   10   Excellent

Price-to-Value Ratio: Poor   1   2   3   4   5   6   7   8   9   10   Excellent

Aromas and Tastes: _____

_____

Comments on Vintage, Region, Winemaker: _____

_____

Recommended		Not Recommended
	(Circle One)	

WINE: _____ Vintage: _____ Producer: _____

Region/Country: _____ Price: _____ Date Tasted: _____

Grape(s): _____

Importer/Distributor: _____ Alcohol % _____

CIRCLE YOUR RATINGS BELOW.

Color/Style: Red   White   Rosé   Sparkling   Effervescent   Fortified

Appearance: Thin   Translucent   Saturated   Opaque

Dry/Sweet Spectrum: Dry   1   2   3   4   5   6   7   8   9   10   Sweet

Body: Light   Light to Medium   Medium   Medium to Full   Full

Balance: Unbalanced   1   2   3   4   5   6   7   8   9   10   Balanced

Finish: Short   Short to Medium   Medium   Medium to Long   Long

Overall Tasting Experience: Poor   1   2   3   4   5   6   7   8   9   10   Excellent

Price-to-Value Ratio: Poor   1   2   3   4   5   6   7   8   9   10   Excellent

Aromas and Tastes: _____

_____

Comments on Vintage, Region, Winemaker: _____

_____

Recommended   Not Recommended

(*Circle One*)

108

WINE: _____ Vintage: _____ Producer: _____

Region/Country: _____ Price: _____ Date Tasted: _____

Grape(s): _____

Importer/Distributor: _____ Alcohol % _____

CIRCLE YOUR RATINGS BELOW.

Color/Style: Red White Rosé Sparkling Effervescent Fortified

Appearance: Thin Translucent Saturated Opaque

Dry/Sweet Spectrum: Dry 1 2 3 4 5 6 7 8 9 10 Sweet

Body: Light Light to Medium Medium Medium to Full Full

Balance: Unbalanced 1 2 3 4 5 6 7 8 9 10 Balanced

Finish: Short Short to Medium Medium Medium to Long Long

Overall Tasting Experience: Poor 1 2 3 4 5 6 7 8 9 10 Excellent

Price-to-Value Ratio: Poor 1 2 3 4 5 6 7 8 9 10 Excellent

Aromas and Tastes: _____

_____

Comments on Vintage, Region, Winemaker: _____

_____

Recommended	Not Recommended
	(Circle One)	

WINE: _____ Vintage: _____ Producer: _____

Region/Country: _____ Price: _____ Date Tasted: _____

Grape(s): _____

Importer/Distributor: _____ Alcohol % _____

CIRCLE YOUR RATINGS BELOW.

Color/Style: Red   White   Rosé   Sparkling   Effervescent   Fortified

Appearance: Thin   Translucent   Saturated   Opaque

Dry/Sweet Spectrum: Dry   1   2   3   4   5   6   7   8   9   10   Sweet

Body: Light   Light to Medium   Medium   Medium to Full   Full

Balance: Unbalanced   1   2   3   4   5   6   7   8   9   10   Balanced

Finish: Short   Short to Medium   Medium   Medium to Long   Long

Overall Tasting Experience: Poor   1   2   3   4   5   6   7   8   9   10   Excellent

Price-to-Value Ratio: Poor   1   2   3   4   5   6   7   8   9   10   Excellent

Aromas and Tastes: _____

_____

Comments on Vintage, Region, Winemaker: _____

_____

Recommended   Not Recommended
            (*Circle One*)

WINE: _____ Vintage: _____ Producer: _____

Region/Country: _____ Price: _____ Date Tasted: _____

Grape(s): _____

Importer/Distributor: _____ Alcohol % _____

CIRCLE YOUR RATINGS BELOW.

Color/Style: Red   White   Rosé   Sparkling   Effervescent   Fortified

Appearance: Thin   Translucent   Saturated   Opaque

Dry/Sweet Spectrum: Dry   1   2   3   4   5   6   7   8   9   10   Sweet

Body: Light   Light to Medium   Medium   Medium to Full   Full

Balance: Unbalanced   1   2   3   4   5   6   7   8   9   10   Balanced

Finish: Short   Short to Medium   Medium   Medium to Long   Long

Overall Tasting Experience: Poor   1   2   3   4   5   6   7   8   9   10   Excellent

Price-to-Value Ratio: Poor   1   2   3   4   5   6   7   8   9   10   Excellent

Aromas and Tastes: _____

_____

Comments on Vintage, Region, Winemaker: _____

_____

Recommended   Not Recommended
                    (*Circle One*)

WINE: _____ Vintage: _____ Producer: _____

Region/Country: _____ Price: _____ Date Tasted: _____

Grape(s): _____

Importer/Distributor: _____ Alcohol % _____

CIRCLE YOUR RATINGS BELOW.

Color/Style: Red   White   Rosé   Sparkling   Effervescent   Fortified

Appearance: Thin   Translucent   Saturated   Opaque

Dry/Sweet Spectrum: Dry   1   2   3   4   5   6   7   8   9   10   Sweet

Body: Light   Light to Medium   Medium   Medium to Full   Full

Balance: Unbalanced   1   2   3   4   5   6   7   8   9   10   Balanced

Finish: Short   Short to Medium   Medium   Medium to Long   Long

Overall Tasting Experience: Poor   1   2   3   4   5   6   7   8   9   10   Excellent

Price-to-Value Ratio: Poor   1   2   3   4   5   6   7   8   9   10   Excellent

Aromas and Tastes: _____

_____

Comments on Vintage, Region, Winemaker: _____

_____

Recommended   Not Recommended
                    (*Circle One*)

WINE: .... Vintage:.............. Producer:...

Region/Country: .... Price: .... Date Tasted:..............

Grape(s): ....

Importer/Distributor: .... Alcohol % ....

CIRCLE YOUR RATINGS BELOW.

Color/Style: Red   White   Rosé   Sparkling   Effervescent   Fortified

Appearance: Thin   Translucent   Saturated   Opaque

Dry/Sweet Spectrum: Dry   1   2   3   4   5   6   7   8   9   10   Sweet

Body: Light   Light to Medium   Medium   Medium to Full   Full

Balance: Unbalanced   1   2   3   4   5   6   7   8   9   10   Balanced

Finish: Short   Short to Medium   Medium   Medium to Long   Long

Overall Tasting Experience: Poor   1   2   3   4   5   6   7   8   9   10   Excellent

Price-to-Value Ratio: Poor   1   2   3   4   5   6   7   8   9   10   Excellent

Aromas and Tastes: ....

....

Comments on Vintage, Region, Winemaker: ....

....

Recommended		Not Recommended
	(*Circle One*)	

WINE: _____ Vintage: _____ Producer: _____

Region/Country: _____ Price: _____ Date Tasted: _____

Grape(s): _____

Importer/Distributor: _____ Alcohol % _____

CIRCLE YOUR RATINGS BELOW.

Color/Style: Red White Rosé Sparkling Effervescent Fortified

Appearance: Thin Translucent Saturated Opaque

Dry/Sweet Spectrum: Dry 1 2 3 4 5 6 7 8 9 10 Sweet

Body: Light Light to Medium Medium Medium to Full Full

Balance: Unbalanced 1 2 3 4 5 6 7 8 9 10 Balanced

Finish: Short Short to Medium Medium Medium to Long Long

Overall Tasting Experience: Poor 1 2 3 4 5 6 7 8 9 10 Excellent

Price-to-Value Ratio: Poor 1 2 3 4 5 6 7 8 9 10 Excellent

Aromas and Tastes: _____

_____

Comments on Vintage, Region, Winemaker: _____

_____

| Recommended | Not Recommended |
| *(Circle One)* |

WINE: _____ Vintage: _____ Producer: _____

Region/Country: _____ Price: _____ Date Tasted: _____

Grape(s): _____

Importer/Distributor: _____ Alcohol % _____

CIRCLE YOUR RATINGS BELOW.

Color/Style: Red White Rosé Sparkling Effervescent Fortified

Appearance: Thin Translucent Saturated Opaque

Dry/Sweet Spectrum: Dry 1 2 3 4 5 6 7 8 9 10 Sweet

Body: Light Light to Medium Medium Medium to Full Full

Balance: Unbalanced 1 2 3 4 5 6 7 8 9 10 Balanced

Finish: Short Short to Medium Medium Medium to Long Long

Overall Tasting Experience: Poor 1 2 3 4 5 6 7 8 9 10 Excellent

Price-to-Value Ratio: Poor 1 2 3 4 5 6 7 8 9 10 Excellent

Aromas and Tastes: _____

_____

Comments on Vintage, Region, Winemaker: _____

_____

Recommended		Not Recommended
	(*Circle One*)	

WINE: _____ Vintage: _____ Producer: _____

Region/Country: _____ Price: _____ Date Tasted: _____

Grape(s): _____

Importer/Distributor: _____ Alcohol % _____

CIRCLE YOUR RATINGS BELOW.

Color/Style: Red White Rosé Sparkling Effervescent Fortified

Appearance: Thin Translucent Saturated Opaque

Dry/Sweet Spectrum: Dry 1 2 3 4 5 6 7 8 9 10 Sweet

Body: Light Light to Medium Medium Medium to Full Full

Balance: Unbalanced 1 2 3 4 5 6 7 8 9 10 Balanced

Finish: Short Short to Medium Medium Medium to Long Long

Overall Tasting Experience: Poor 1 2 3 4 5 6 7 8 9 10 Excellent

Price-to-Value Ratio: Poor 1 2 3 4 5 6 7 8 9 10 Excellent

Aromas and Tastes: _____

_____

Comments on Vintage, Region, Winemaker: _____

_____

Recommended	Not Recommended
	(Circle One)

WINE: _____ Vintage: _____ Producer: _____

Region/Country: _____ Price: _____ Date Tasted: _____

Grape(s): _____

Importer/Distributor: _____ Alcohol % _____

Color/Style: Red White Rosé Sparkling Effervescent Fortified

Appearance: Thin Translucent Saturated Opaque

Dry/Sweet Spectrum: Dry 1 2 3 4 5 6 7 8 9 10 Sweet

Body: Light Light to Medium Medium Medium to Full Full

Balance: Unbalanced 1 2 3 4 5 6 7 8 9 10 Balanced

Finish: Short Short to Medium Medium Medium to Long Long

Overall Tasting Experience: Poor 1 2 3 4 5 6 7 8 9 10 Excellent

Price-to-Value Ratio: Poor 1 2 3 4 5 6 7 8 9 10 Excellent

Aromas and Tastes: _____

_____

Comments on Vintage, Region, Winemaker: _____

_____

Recommended   Not Recommended

(*Circle One*)

WINE: _____ Vintage: _____ Producer: _____

Region/Country: _____ Price: _____ Date Tasted: _____

Grape(s): _____

Importer/Distributor: _____ Alcohol % _____

CIRCLE YOUR RATINGS BELOW.

Color/Style: Red White Rosé Sparkling Effervescent Fortified

Appearance: Thin Translucent Saturated Opaque

Dry/Sweet Spectrum: Dry 1 2 3 4 5 6 7 8 9 10 Sweet

Body: Light Light to Medium Medium Medium to Full Full

Balance: Unbalanced 1 2 3 4 5 6 7 8 9 10 Balanced

Finish: Short Short to Medium Medium Medium to Long Long

Overall Tasting Experience: Poor 1 2 3 4 5 6 7 8 9 10 Excellent

Price-to-Value Ratio: Poor 1 2 3 4 5 6 7 8 9 10 Excellent

Aromas and Tastes: _____

_____

Comments on Vintage, Region, Winemaker: _____

_____

Recommended   Not Recommended
               (*Circle One*)

WINE: .... Vintage: .... Producer: ....

Region/Country: .... Price: .... Date Tasted: ....

Grape(s): ....

Importer/Distributor: .... Alcohol % ....

CIRCLE YOUR RATINGS BELOW.

Color/Style: Red   White   Rosé   Sparkling   Effervescent   Fortified

Appearance: Thin   Translucent   Saturated   Opaque

Dry/Sweet Spectrum: Dry   1   2   3   4   5   6   7   8   9   10   Sweet

Body: Light   Light to Medium   Medium   Medium to Full   Full

Balance: Unbalanced   1   2   3   4   5   6   7   8   9   10   Balanced

Finish: Short   Short to Medium   Medium   Medium to Long   Long

Overall Tasting Experience: Poor   1   2   3   4   5   6   7   8   9   10   Excellent

Price-to-Value Ratio: Poor   1   2   3   4   5   6   7   8   9   10   Excellent

Aromas and Tastes: ....

....

Comments on Vintage, Region, Winemaker: ....

....

Recommended	Not Recommended

(Circle One)

WINE: _____ Vintage: _____ Producer: _____

Region/Country: _____ Price: _____ Date Tasted: _____

Grape(s): _____

Importer/Distributor: _____ Alcohol % _____

CIRCLE YOUR RATINGS BELOW.

Color/Style: Red White Rosé Sparkling Effervescent Fortified

Appearance: Thin Translucent Saturated Opaque

Dry/Sweet Spectrum: Dry 1 2 3 4 5 6 7 8 9 10 Sweet

Body: Light Light to Medium Medium Medium to Full Full

Balance: Unbalanced 1 2 3 4 5 6 7 8 9 10 Balanced

Finish: Short Short to Medium Medium Medium to Long Long

Overall Tasting Experience: Poor 1 2 3 4 5 6 7 8 9 10 Excellent

Price-to-Value Ratio: Poor 1 2 3 4 5 6 7 8 9 10 Excellent

Aromas and Tastes: _____

_____

Comments on Vintage, Region, Winemaker: _____

_____

Recommended   Not Recommended
            (Circle One)

WINE: _____ Vintage: _____ Producer: _____

Region/Country: _____ Price: _____ Date Tasted: _____

Grape(s): _____

Importer/Distributor: _____ Alcohol % _____

CIRCLE YOUR RATINGS BELOW.

Color/Style: Red   White   Rosé   Sparkling   Effervescent   Fortified

Appearance: Thin   Translucent   Saturated   Opaque

Dry/Sweet Spectrum: Dry   1   2   3   4   5   6   7   8   9   10   Sweet

Body: Light   Light to Medium   Medium   Medium to Full   Full

Balance: Unbalanced   1   2   3   4   5   6   7   8   9   10   Balanced

Finish: Short   Short to Medium   Medium   Medium to Long   Long

Overall Tasting Experience: Poor   1   2   3   4   5   6   7   8   9   10   Excellent

Price-to-Value Ratio: Poor   1   2   3   4   5   6   7   8   9   10   Excellent

Aromas and Tastes: _____

_____

Comments on Vintage, Region, Winemaker: _____

_____

Recommended	Not Recommended
(Circle One)	

WINE: _____ Vintage: _____ Producer: _____

Region/Country: _____ Price: _____ Date Tasted: _____

Grape(s): _____

Importer/Distributor: _____ Alcohol % _____

CIRCLE YOUR RATINGS BELOW.

Color/Style: Red White Rosé Sparkling Effervescent Fortified

Appearance: Thin Translucent Saturated Opaque

Dry/Sweet Spectrum: Dry 1 2 3 4 5 6 7 8 9 10 Sweet

Body: Light Light to Medium Medium Medium to Full Full

Balance: Unbalanced 1 2 3 4 5 6 7 8 9 10 Balanced

Finish: Short Short to Medium Medium Medium to Long Long

Overall Tasting Experience: Poor 1 2 3 4 5 6 7 8 9 10 Excellent

Price-to-Value Ratio: Poor 1 2 3 4 5 6 7 8 9 10 Excellent

Aromas and Tastes: _____

_____

Comments on Vintage, Region, Winemaker: _____

_____

Recommended   Not Recommended

(*Circle One*)

WINE: _____ Vintage: _____ Producer: _____

Region/Country: _____ Price: _____ Date Tasted: _____

Grape(s): _____

Importer/Distributor: _____ Alcohol % _____

CIRCLE YOUR RATINGS BELOW.

Color/Style: Red White Rosé Sparkling Effervescent Fortified

Appearance: Thin Translucent Saturated Opaque

Dry/Sweet Spectrum: Dry 1 2 3 4 5 6 7 8 9 10 Sweet

Body: Light Light to Medium Medium Medium to Full Full

Balance: Unbalanced 1 2 3 4 5 6 7 8 9 10 Balanced

Finish: Short Short to Medium Medium Medium to Long Long

Overall Tasting Experience: Poor 1 2 3 4 5 6 7 8 9 10 Excellent

Price-to-Value Ratio: Poor 1 2 3 4 5 6 7 8 9 10 Excellent

Aromas and Tastes: _____

_____

Comments on Vintage, Region, Winemaker: _____

_____

Recommended   Not Recommended
                    (Circle One)

123

WINE: _____ Vintage: _____ Producer: _____

Region/Country: _____ Price: _____ Date Tasted: _____

Grape(s): _____

Importer/Distributor: _____ Alcohol % _____

CIRCLE YOUR RATINGS BELOW.

Color/Style: Red White Rosé Sparkling Effervescent Fortified

Appearance: Thin Translucent Saturated Opaque

Dry/Sweet Spectrum: Dry 1 2 3 4 5 6 7 8 9 10 Sweet

Body: Light Light to Medium Medium Medium to Full Full

Balance: Unbalanced 1 2 3 4 5 6 7 8 9 10 Balanced

Finish: Short Short to Medium Medium Medium to Long Long

Overall Tasting Experience: Poor 1 2 3 4 5 6 7 8 9 10 Excellent

Price-to-Value Ratio: Poor 1 2 3 4 5 6 7 8 9 10 Excellent

Aromas and Tastes: _____

_____

Comments on Vintage, Region, Winemaker: _____

_____

Recommended		Not Recommended
	(Circle One)	

WINE: _____ Vintage: _____ Producer: _____

Region/Country: _____ Price: _____ Date Tasted: _____

Grape(s): _____

Importer/Distributor: _____ Alcohol % _____

CIRCLE YOUR RATINGS BELOW.

Color/Style: Red White Rosé Sparkling Effervescent Fortified

Appearance: Thin Translucent Saturated Opaque

Dry/Sweet Spectrum: Dry 1 2 3 4 5 6 7 8 9 10 Sweet

Body: Light Light to Medium Medium Medium to Full Full

Balance: Unbalanced 1 2 3 4 5 6 7 8 9 10 Balanced

Finish: Short Short to Medium Medium Medium to Long Long

Overall Tasting Experience: Poor 1 2 3 4 5 6 7 8 9 10 Excellent

Price-to-Value Ratio: Poor 1 2 3 4 5 6 7 8 9 10 Excellent

Aromas and Tastes: _____

_____

Comments on Vintage, Region, Winemaker: _____

_____

Recommended	Not Recommended

(*Circle One*)

WINE: _____ Vintage: _____ Producer: _____

Region/Country: _____ Price: _____ Date Tasted: _____

Grape(s): _____

Importer/Distributor: _____ Alcohol % _____

CIRCLE YOUR RATINGS BELOW.

Color/Style: Red White Rosé Sparkling Effervescent Fortified

Appearance: Thin Translucent Saturated Opaque

Dry/Sweet Spectrum: Dry 1 2 3 4 5 6 7 8 9 10 Sweet

Body: Light Light to Medium Medium Medium to Full Full

Balance: Unbalanced 1 2 3 4 5 6 7 8 9 10 Balanced

Finish: Short Short to Medium Medium Medium to Long Long

Overall Tasting Experience: Poor 1 2 3 4 5 6 7 8 9 10 Excellent

Price-to-Value Ratio: Poor 1 2 3 4 5 6 7 8 9 10 Excellent

Aromas and Tastes: _____

_____

Comments on Vintage, Region, Winemaker: _____

_____

Recommended		Not Recommended
	(Circle One)	

WINE: _____ Vintage: _____ Producer: _____

Region/Country: _____ Price: _____ Date Tasted: _____

Grape(s): _____

Importer/Distributor: _____ Alcohol % _____

CIRCLE YOUR RATINGS BELOW.

Color/Style: Red   White   Rosé   Sparkling   Effervescent   Fortified

Appearance: Thin   Translucent   Saturated   Opaque

Dry/Sweet Spectrum: Dry   1   2   3   4   5   6   7   8   9   10   Sweet

Body: Light   Light to Medium   Medium   Medium to Full   Full

Balance: Unbalanced   1   2   3   4   5   6   7   8   9   10   Balanced

Finish: Short   Short to Medium   Medium   Medium to Long   Long

Overall Tasting Experience: Poor   1   2   3   4   5   6   7   8   9   10   Excellent

Price-to-Value Ratio: Poor   1   2   3   4   5   6   7   8   9   10   Excellent

Aromas and Tastes: _____

_____

Comments on Vintage, Region, Winemaker: _____

_____

Recommended	Not Recommended
(Circle One)	

WINE: _____ Vintage: _____ Producer: _____

Region/Country: _____ Price: _____ Date Tasted: _____

Grape(s): _____

Importer/Distributor: _____ Alcohol % _____

CIRCLE YOUR RATINGS BELOW.

Color/Style: Red White Rosé Sparkling Effervescent Fortified

Appearance: Thin Translucent Saturated Opaque

Dry/Sweet Spectrum: Dry 1 2 3 4 5 6 7 8 9 10 Sweet

Body: Light Light to Medium Medium Medium to Full Full

Balance: Unbalanced 1 2 3 4 5 6 7 8 9 10 Balanced

Finish: Short Short to Medium Medium Medium to Long Long

Overall Tasting Experience: Poor 1 2 3 4 5 6 7 8 9 10 Excellent

Price-to-Value Ratio: Poor 1 2 3 4 5 6 7 8 9 10 Excellent

Aromas and Tastes: _____

_____

Comments on Vintage, Region, Winemaker: _____

_____

Recommended   Not Recommended
                  (Circle One)

WINE: _____ Vintage: _____ Producer: _____

Region/Country: _____ Price: _____ Date Tasted: _____

Grape(s): _____

Importer/Distributor: _____ Alcohol % _____

CIRCLE YOUR RATINGS BELOW.

Color/Style: Red White Rosé Sparkling Effervescent Fortified

Appearance: Thin Translucent Saturated Opaque

Dry/Sweet Spectrum: Dry 1 2 3 4 5 6 7 8 9 10 Sweet

Body: Light Light to Medium Medium Medium to Full Full

Balance: Unbalanced 1 2 3 4 5 6 7 8 9 10 Balanced

Finish: Short Short to Medium Medium Medium to Long Long

Overall Tasting Experience: Poor 1 2 3 4 5 6 7 8 9 10 Excellent

Price-to-Value Ratio: Poor 1 2 3 4 5 6 7 8 9 10 Excellent

Aromas and Tastes: _____

_____

Comments on Vintage, Region, Winemaker: _____

_____

Recommended	Not Recommended

(Circle One)

129

WINE: _____ Vintage: _____ Producer: _____

Region/Country: _____ Price: _____ Date Tasted: _____

Grape(s): _____

Importer/Distributor: _____ Alcohol % _____

CIRCLE YOUR RATINGS BELOW.

Color/Style: Red   White   Rosé   Sparkling   Effervescent   Fortified

Appearance: Thin   Translucent   Saturated   Opaque

Dry/Sweet Spectrum: Dry   1   2   3   4   5   6   7   8   9   10   Sweet

Body: Light   Light to Medium   Medium   Medium to Full   Full

Balance: Unbalanced   1   2   3   4   5   6   7   8   9   10   Balanced

Finish: Short   Short to Medium   Medium   Medium to Long   Long

Overall Tasting Experience: Poor   1   2   3   4   5   6   7   8   9   10   Excellent

Price-to-Value Ratio: Poor   1   2   3   4   5   6   7   8   9   10   Excellent

Aromas and Tastes: _____

_____

Comments on Vintage, Region, Winemaker: _____

_____

Recommended		Not Recommended
	(Circle One)	

WINE: _____ Vintage: _____ Producer: _____

Region/Country: _____ Price: _____ Date Tasted: _____

Grape(s): _____

Importer/Distributor: _____ Alcohol % _____

CIRCLE YOUR RATINGS BELOW.

Color/Style: Red White Rosé Sparkling Effervescent Fortified

Appearance: Thin Translucent Saturated Opaque

Dry/Sweet Spectrum: Dry 1 2 3 4 5 6 7 8 9 10 Sweet

Body: Light Light to Medium Medium Medium to Full Full

Balance: Unbalanced 1 2 3 4 5 6 7 8 9 10 Balanced

Finish: Short Short to Medium Medium Medium to Long Long

Overall Tasting Experience: Poor 1 2 3 4 5 6 7 8 9 10 Excellent

Price-to-Value Ratio: Poor 1 2 3 4 5 6 7 8 9 10 Excellent

Aromas and Tastes: _____

_____

Comments on Vintage, Region, Winemaker: _____

_____

Recommended	Not Recommended

(*Circle One*)

WINE: _____ Vintage: _____ Producer: _____

Region/Country: _____ Price: _____ Date Tasted: _____

Grape(s): _____

Importer/Distributor: _____ Alcohol % _____

CIRCLE YOUR RATINGS BELOW.

Color/Style: Red White Rosé Sparkling Effervescent Fortified

Appearance: Thin Translucent Saturated Opaque

Dry/Sweet Spectrum: Dry 1 2 3 4 5 6 7 8 9 10 Sweet

Body: Light Light to Medium Medium Medium to Full Full

Balance: Unbalanced 1 2 3 4 5 6 7 8 9 10 Balanced

Finish: Short Short to Medium Medium Medium to Long Long

Overall Tasting Experience: Poor 1 2 3 4 5 6 7 8 9 10 Excellent

Price-to-Value Ratio: Poor 1 2 3 4 5 6 7 8 9 10 Excellent

Aromas and Tastes: _____

_____

Comments on Vintage, Region, Winemaker: _____

_____

Recommended   Not Recommended

(*Circle One*)

WINE: _____ Vintage: _____ Producer: _____

Region/Country: _____ Price: _____ Date Tasted: _____

Grape(s): _____

Importer/Distributor: _____ Alcohol % _____

CIRCLE YOUR RATINGS BELOW.

Color/Style: Red White Rosé Sparkling Effervescent Fortified

Appearance: Thin Translucent Saturated Opaque

Dry/Sweet Spectrum: Dry 1 2 3 4 5 6 7 8 9 10 Sweet

Body: Light Light to Medium Medium Medium to Full Full

Balance: Unbalanced 1 2 3 4 5 6 7 8 9 10 Balanced

Finish: Short Short to Medium Medium Medium to Long Long

Overall Tasting Experience: Poor 1 2 3 4 5 6 7 8 9 10 Excellent

Price-to-Value Ratio: Poor 1 2 3 4 5 6 7 8 9 10 Excellent

Aromas and Tastes: _____

_____

Comments on Vintage, Region, Winemaker: _____

_____

Recommended		Not Recommended
	(Circle One)	

WINE: _____ Vintage: _____ Producer: _____

Region/Country: _____ Price: _____ Date Tasted: _____

Grape(s): _____

Importer/Distributor: _____ Alcohol % _____

CIRCLE YOUR RATINGS BELOW.

Color/Style: Red White Rosé Sparkling Effervescent Fortified

Appearance: Thin Translucent Saturated Opaque

Dry/Sweet Spectrum: Dry 1 2 3 4 5 6 7 8 9 10 Sweet

Body: Light Light to Medium Medium Medium to Full Full

Balance: Unbalanced 1 2 3 4 5 6 7 8 9 10 Balanced

Finish: Short Short to Medium Medium Medium to Long Long

Overall Tasting Experience: Poor 1 2 3 4 5 6 7 8 9 10 Excellent

Price-to-Value Ratio: Poor 1 2 3 4 5 6 7 8 9 10 Excellent

Aromas and Tastes: _____

_____

Comments on Vintage, Region, Winemaker: _____

_____

Recommended   Not Recommended

(Circle One)

WINE: _____ Vintage: _____ Producer: _____

Region/Country: _____ Price: _____ Date Tasted: _____

Grape(s): _____

Importer/Distributor: _____ Alcohol % _____

CIRCLE YOUR RATINGS BELOW.

Color/Style: Red   White   Rosé   Sparkling   Effervescent   Fortified

Appearance: Thin   Translucent   Saturated   Opaque

Dry/Sweet Spectrum: Dry   1   2   3   4   5   6   7   8   9   10   Sweet

Body: Light   Light to Medium   Medium   Medium to Full   Full

Balance: Unbalanced   1   2   3   4   5   6   7   8   9   10   Balanced

Finish: Short   Short to Medium   Medium   Medium to Long   Long

Overall Tasting Experience: Poor   1   2   3   4   5   6   7   8   9   10   Excellent

Price-to-Value Ratio: Poor   1   2   3   4   5   6   7   8   9   10   Excellent

Aromas and Tastes: _____

_____

Comments on Vintage, Region, Winemaker: _____

_____

Recommended   Not Recommended

(Circle One)

135

WINE: _____ Vintage: _____ Producer: _____

Region/Country: _____ Price: _____ Date Tasted: _____

Grape(s): _____

Importer/Distributor: _____ Alcohol % _____

CIRCLE YOUR RATINGS BELOW.

Color/Style: Red   White   Rosé   Sparkling   Effervescent   Fortified

Appearance: Thin   Translucent   Saturated   Opaque

Dry/Sweet Spectrum: Dry   1   2   3   4   5   6   7   8   9   10   Sweet

Body: Light   Light to Medium   Medium   Medium to Full   Full

Balance: Unbalanced   1   2   3   4   5   6   7   8   9   10   Balanced

Finish: Short   Short to Medium   Medium   Medium to Long   Long

Overall Tasting Experience: Poor   1   2   3   4   5   6   7   8   9   10   Excellent

Price-to-Value Ratio: Poor   1   2   3   4   5   6   7   8   9   10   Excellent

Aromas and Tastes: _____

_____

Comments on Vintage, Region, Winemaker: _____

_____

Recommended   Not Recommended
                  (*Circle One*)

WINE: _____ Vintage: _____ Producer: _____

Region/Country: _____ Price: _____ Date Tasted: _____

Grape(s): _____

Importer/Distributor: _____ Alcohol % _____

CIRCLE YOUR RATINGS BELOW.

Color/Style: Red   White   Rosé   Sparkling   Effervescent   Fortified

Appearance: Thin   Translucent   Saturated   Opaque

Dry/Sweet Spectrum: Dry   1   2   3   4   5   6   7   8   9   10   Sweet

Body: Light   Light to Medium   Medium   Medium to Full   Full

Balance: Unbalanced   1   2   3   4   5   6   7   8   9   10   Balanced

Finish: Short   Short to Medium   Medium   Medium to Long   Long

Overall Tasting Experience: Poor   1   2   3   4   5   6   7   8   9   10   Excellent

Price-to-Value Ratio: Poor   1   2   3   4   5   6   7   8   9   10   Excellent

Aromas and Tastes: _____

_____

Comments on Vintage, Region, Winemaker: _____

_____

| Recommended | Not Recommended |
| *(Circle One)* |

137

WINE: _____ Vintage: _____ Producer: _____

Region/Country: _____ Price: _____ Date Tasted: _____

Grape(s): _____

Importer/Distributor: _____ Alcohol % _____

CIRCLE YOUR RATINGS BELOW.

Color/Style: Red White Rosé Sparkling Effervescent Fortified

Appearance: Thin Translucent Saturated Opaque

Dry/Sweet Spectrum: Dry 1 2 3 4 5 6 7 8 9 10 Sweet

Body: Light Light to Medium Medium Medium to Full Full

Balance: Unbalanced 1 2 3 4 5 6 7 8 9 10 Balanced

Finish: Short Short to Medium Medium Medium to Long Long

Overall Tasting Experience: Poor 1 2 3 4 5 6 7 8 9 10 Excellent

Price-to-Value Ratio: Poor 1 2 3 4 5 6 7 8 9 10 Excellent

Aromas and Tastes: _____

_____

Comments on Vintage, Region, Winemaker: _____

_____

Recommended		Not Recommended
	(Circle One)	

WINE: _____ Vintage: _____ Producer: _____

Region/Country: _____ Price: _____ Date Tasted: _____

Grape(s): _____

Importer/Distributor: _____ Alcohol % _____

CIRCLE YOUR RATINGS BELOW.

Color/Style: Red White Rosé Sparkling Effervescent Fortified

Appearance: Thin Translucent Saturated Opaque

Dry/Sweet Spectrum: Dry 1 2 3 4 5 6 7 8 9 10 Sweet

Body: Light Light to Medium Medium Medium to Full Full

Balance: Unbalanced 1 2 3 4 5 6 7 8 9 10 Balanced

Finish: Short Short to Medium Medium Medium to Long Long

Overall Tasting Experience: Poor 1 2 3 4 5 6 7 8 9 10 Excellent

Price-to-Value Ratio: Poor 1 2 3 4 5 6 7 8 9 10 Excellent

Aromas and Tastes: _____

_____

Comments on Vintage, Region, Winemaker: _____

_____

Recommended   Not Recommended
                  (*Circle One*)

WINE: _____ Vintage: _____ Producer: _____

Region/Country: _____ Price: _____ Date Tasted: _____

Grape(s): _____

Importer/Distributor: _____ Alcohol % _____

CIRCLE YOUR RATINGS BELOW.

Color/Style: Red White Rosé Sparkling Effervescent Fortified

Appearance: Thin Translucent Saturated Opaque

Dry/Sweet Spectrum: Dry 1 2 3 4 5 6 7 8 9 10 Sweet

Body: Light Light to Medium Medium Medium to Full Full

Balance: Unbalanced 1 2 3 4 5 6 7 8 9 10 Balanced

Finish: Short Short to Medium Medium Medium to Long Long

Overall Tasting Experience: Poor 1 2 3 4 5 6 7 8 9 10 Excellent

Price-to-Value Ratio: Poor 1 2 3 4 5 6 7 8 9 10 Excellent

Aromas and Tastes: _____

_____

Comments on Vintage, Region, Winemaker: _____

_____

Recommended   Not Recommended
                    (*Circle One*)

WINE: .... Vintage: .... Producer: ....

Region/Country: .... Price: .... Date Tasted: ....

Grape(s): ....

Importer/Distributor: .... Alcohol % ....

CIRCLE YOUR RATINGS BELOW.

Color/Style: Red White Rosé Sparkling Effervescent Fortified

Appearance: Thin Translucent Saturated Opaque

Dry/Sweet Spectrum: Dry 1 2 3 4 5 6 7 8 9 10 Sweet

Body: Light Light to Medium Medium Medium to Full Full

Balance: Unbalanced 1 2 3 4 5 6 7 8 9 10 Balanced

Finish: Short Short to Medium Medium Medium to Long Long

Overall Tasting Experience: Poor 1 2 3 4 5 6 7 8 9 10 Excellent

Price-to-Value Ratio: Poor 1 2 3 4 5 6 7 8 9 10 Excellent

Aromas and Tastes: ....

....

Comments on Vintage, Region, Winemaker: ....

....

Recommended   Not Recommended

(Circle One)

WINE: _____ Vintage: _____ Producer: _____

Region/Country: _____ Price: _____ Date Tasted: _____

Grape(s): _____

Importer/Distributor: _____ Alcohol % _____

CIRCLE YOUR RATINGS BELOW.

Color/Style: Red White Rosé Sparkling Effervescent Fortified

Appearance: Thin Translucent Saturated Opaque

Dry/Sweet Spectrum: Dry 1 2 3 4 5 6 7 8 9 10 Sweet

Body: Light Light to Medium Medium Medium to Full Full

Balance: Unbalanced 1 2 3 4 5 6 7 8 9 10 Balanced

Finish: Short Short to Medium Medium Medium to Long Long

Overall Tasting Experience: Poor 1 2 3 4 5 6 7 8 9 10 Excellent

Price-to-Value Ratio: Poor 1 2 3 4 5 6 7 8 9 10 Excellent

Aromas and Tastes: _____

_____

Comments on Vintage, Region, Winemaker: _____

_____

Recommended		Not Recommended
	(Circle One)	

WINE: _____ Vintage: _____ Producer: _____

Region/Country: _____ Price: _____ Date Tasted: _____

Grape(s): _____

Importer/Distributor: _____ Alcohol % _____

CIRCLE YOUR RATINGS BELOW.

Color/Style: Red   White   Rosé   Sparkling   Effervescent   Fortified

Appearance: Thin   Translucent   Saturated   Opaque

Dry/Sweet Spectrum: Dry   1   2   3   4   5   6   7   8   9   10   Sweet

Body: Light   Light to Medium   Medium   Medium to Full   Full

Balance: Unbalanced   1   2   3   4   5   6   7   8   9   10   Balanced

Finish: Short   Short to Medium   Medium   Medium to Long   Long

Overall Tasting Experience: Poor   1   2   3   4   5   6   7   8   9   10   Excellent

Price-to-Value Ratio: Poor   1   2   3   4   5   6   7   8   9   10   Excellent

Aromas and Tastes: _____

_____

Comments on Vintage, Region, Winemaker: _____

_____

Recommended   Not Recommended
                    (*Circle One*)

WINE: _____ Vintage: _____ Producer: _____

Region/Country: _____ Price: _____ Date Tasted: _____

Grape(s): _____

Importer/Distributor: _____ Alcohol % _____

CIRCLE YOUR RATINGS BELOW.

Color/Style: Red White Rosé Sparkling Effervescent Fortified

Appearance: Thin Translucent Saturated Opaque

Dry/Sweet Spectrum: Dry 1 2 3 4 5 6 7 8 9 10 Sweet

Body: Light Light to Medium Medium Medium to Full Full

Balance: Unbalanced 1 2 3 4 5 6 7 8 9 10 Balanced

Finish: Short Short to Medium Medium Medium to Long Long

Overall Tasting Experience: Poor 1 2 3 4 5 6 7 8 9 10 Excellent

Price-to-Value Ratio: Poor 1 2 3 4 5 6 7 8 9 10 Excellent

Aromas and Tastes: _____

_____

Comments on Vintage, Region, Winemaker: _____

_____

Recommended   Not Recommended
                (Circle One)

WINE: _____ Vintage: _____ Producer: _____

Region/Country: _____ Price: _____ Date Tasted: _____

Grape(s): _____

Importer/Distributor: _____ Alcohol % _____

CIRCLE YOUR RATINGS BELOW.

Color/Style: Red   White   Rosé   Sparkling   Effervescent   Fortified

Appearance: Thin   Translucent   Saturated   Opaque

Dry/Sweet Spectrum: Dry   1   2   3   4   5   6   7   8   9   10   Sweet

Body: Light   Light to Medium   Medium   Medium to Full   Full

Balance: Unbalanced   1   2   3   4   5   6   7   8   9   10   Balanced

Finish: Short   Short to Medium   Medium   Medium to Long   Long

Overall Tasting Experience: Poor   1   2   3   4   5   6   7   8   9   10   Excellent

Price-to-Value Ratio: Poor   1   2   3   4   5   6   7   8   9   10   Excellent

Aromas and Tastes: _____

_____

Comments on Vintage, Region, Winemaker: _____

_____

Recommended		Not Recommended
	(Circle One)	

WINE: _____ Vintage: _____ Producer: _____

Region/Country: _____ Price: _____ Date Tasted: _____

Grape(s): _____

Importer/Distributor: _____ Alcohol % _____

CIRCLE YOUR RATINGS BELOW.

Color/Style: Red White Rosé Sparkling Effervescent Fortified

Appearance: Thin Translucent Saturated Opaque

Dry/Sweet Spectrum: Dry 1 2 3 4 5 6 7 8 9 10 Sweet

Body: Light Light to Medium Medium Medium to Full Full

Balance: Unbalanced 1 2 3 4 5 6 7 8 9 10 Balanced

Finish: Short Short to Medium Medium Medium to Long Long

Overall Tasting Experience: Poor 1 2 3 4 5 6 7 8 9 10 Excellent

Price-to-Value Ratio: Poor 1 2 3 4 5 6 7 8 9 10 Excellent

Aromas and Tastes: _____

_____

Comments on Vintage, Region, Winemaker: _____

_____

Recommended   Not Recommended
                    (*Circle One*)

WINE: .... Vintage: .... Producer: ....

Region/Country: .... Price: .... Date Tasted: ....

Grape(s): ....

Importer/Distributor: .... Alcohol % ....

Color/Style: Red White Rosé Sparkling Effervescent Fortified

Appearance: Thin Translucent Saturated Opaque

Dry/Sweet Spectrum: Dry 1 2 3 4 5 6 7 8 9 10 Sweet

Body: Light Light to Medium Medium Medium to Full Full

Balance: Unbalanced 1 2 3 4 5 6 7 8 9 10 Balanced

Finish: Short Short to Medium Medium Medium to Long Long

Overall Tasting Experience: Poor 1 2 3 4 5 6 7 8 9 10 Excellent

Price-to-Value Ratio: Poor 1 2 3 4 5 6 7 8 9 10 Excellent

Aromas and Tastes: ....

....

Comments on Vintage, Region, Winemaker: ....

....

Recommended		Not Recommended
	(Circle One)	

WINE: _____ Vintage: _____ Producer: _____

Region/Country: _____ Price: _____ Date Tasted: _____

Grape(s): _____

Importer/Distributor: _____ Alcohol % _____

CIRCLE YOUR RATINGS BELOW.

Color/Style: Red White Rosé Sparkling Effervescent Fortified

Appearance: Thin Translucent Saturated Opaque

Dry/Sweet Spectrum: Dry 1 2 3 4 5 6 7 8 9 10 Sweet

Body: Light Light to Medium Medium Medium to Full Full

Balance: Unbalanced 1 2 3 4 5 6 7 8 9 10 Balanced

Finish: Short Short to Medium Medium Medium to Long Long

Overall Tasting Experience: Poor 1 2 3 4 5 6 7 8 9 10 Excellent

Price-to-Value Ratio: Poor 1 2 3 4 5 6 7 8 9 10 Excellent

Aromas and Tastes: _____

_____

Comments on Vintage, Region, Winemaker: _____

_____

Recommended   Not Recommended
                (Circle One)

WINE: _____ Vintage: _____ Producer: _____

Region/Country: _____ Price: _____ Date Tasted: _____

Grape(s): _____

Importer/Distributor: _____ Alcohol % _____

CIRCLE YOUR RATINGS BELOW.

Color/Style: Red White Rosé Sparkling Effervescent Fortified

Appearance: Thin Translucent Saturated Opaque

Dry/Sweet Spectrum: Dry 1 2 3 4 5 6 7 8 9 10 Sweet

Body: Light Light to Medium Medium Medium to Full Full

Balance: Unbalanced 1 2 3 4 5 6 7 8 9 10 Balanced

Finish: Short Short to Medium Medium Medium to Long Long

Overall Tasting Experience: Poor 1 2 3 4 5 6 7 8 9 10 Excellent

Price-to-Value Ratio: Poor 1 2 3 4 5 6 7 8 9 10 Excellent

Aromas and Tastes: _____

_____

Comments on Vintage, Region, Winemaker: _____

_____

Recommended   Not Recommended
                    (*Circle One*)

WINE: _____ Vintage: _____ Producer: _____

Region/Country: _____ Price: _____ Date Tasted: _____

Grape(s): _____

Importer/Distributor: _____ Alcohol % _____

CIRCLE YOUR RATINGS BELOW.

Color/Style: Red White Rosé Sparkling Effervescent Fortified

Appearance: Thin Translucent Saturated Opaque

Dry/Sweet Spectrum: Dry 1 2 3 4 5 6 7 8 9 10 Sweet

Body: Light Light to Medium Medium Medium to Full Full

Balance: Unbalanced 1 2 3 4 5 6 7 8 9 10 Balanced

Finish: Short Short to Medium Medium Medium to Long Long

Overall Tasting Experience: Poor 1 2 3 4 5 6 7 8 9 10 Excellent

Price-to-Value Ratio: Poor 1 2 3 4 5 6 7 8 9 10 Excellent

Aromas and Tastes: _____

_____

Comments on Vintage, Region, Winemaker: _____

_____

Recommended   Not Recommended
                  (*Circle One*)

WINE: _____ Vintage: _____ Producer: _____

Region/Country: _____ Price: _____ Date Tasted: _____

Grape(s): _____

Importer/Distributor: _____ Alcohol % _____

CIRCLE YOUR RATINGS BELOW.

Color/Style: Red   White   Rosé   Sparkling   Effervescent   Fortified

Appearance: Thin   Translucent   Saturated   Opaque

Dry/Sweet Spectrum: Dry   1   2   3   4   5   6   7   8   9   10   Sweet

Body: Light   Light to Medium   Medium   Medium to Full   Full

Balance: Unbalanced   1   2   3   4   5   6   7   8   9   10   Balanced

Finish: Short   Short to Medium   Medium   Medium to Long   Long

Overall Tasting Experience: Poor   1   2   3   4   5   6   7   8   9   10   Excellent

Price-to-Value Ratio: Poor   1   2   3   4   5   6   7   8   9   10   Excellent

Aromas and Tastes: _____

_____

Comments on Vintage, Region, Winemaker: _____

_____

Recommended	Not Recommended
(Circle One)	

WINE: _____ Vintage: _____ Producer: _____

Region/Country: _____ Price: _____ Date Tasted: _____

Grape(s): _____

Importer/Distributor: _____ Alcohol % _____

CIRCLE YOUR RATINGS BELOW.

Color/Style: Red White Rosé Sparkling Effervescent Fortified

Appearance: Thin Translucent Saturated Opaque

Dry/Sweet Spectrum: Dry 1 2 3 4 5 6 7 8 9 10 Sweet

Body: Light Light to Medium Medium Medium to Full Full

Balance: Unbalanced 1 2 3 4 5 6 7 8 9 10 Balanced

Finish: Short Short to Medium Medium Medium to Long Long

Overall Tasting Experience: Poor 1 2 3 4 5 6 7 8 9 10 Excellent

Price-to-Value Ratio: Poor 1 2 3 4 5 6 7 8 9 10 Excellent

Aromas and Tastes: _____

_____

Comments on Vintage, Region, Winemaker: _____

_____

Recommended		Not Recommended
	(Circle One)	

WINE: _____ Vintage: _____ Producer: _____

Region/Country: _____ Price: _____ Date Tasted: _____

Grape(s): _____

Importer/Distributor: _____ Alcohol % _____

CIRCLE YOUR RATINGS BELOW.

Color/Style: Red White Rosé Sparkling Effervescent Fortified

Appearance: Thin Translucent Saturated Opaque

Dry/Sweet Spectrum: Dry 1 2 3 4 5 6 7 8 9 10 Sweet

Body: Light Light to Medium Medium Medium to Full Full

Balance: Unbalanced 1 2 3 4 5 6 7 8 9 10 Balanced

Finish: Short Short to Medium Medium Medium to Long Long

Overall Tasting Experience: Poor 1 2 3 4 5 6 7 8 9 10 Excellent

Price-to-Value Ratio: Poor 1 2 3 4 5 6 7 8 9 10 Excellent

Aromas and Tastes: _____

_____

Comments on Vintage, Region, Winemaker: _____

_____

Recommended		Not Recommended
	(Circle One)	

WINE: _____ Vintage: _____ Producer: _____

Region/Country: _____ Price: _____ Date Tasted: _____

Grape(s): _____

Importer/Distributor: _____ Alcohol % _____

CIRCLE YOUR RATINGS BELOW.

Color/Style: Red White Rosé Sparkling Effervescent Fortified

Appearance: Thin Translucent Saturated Opaque

Dry/Sweet Spectrum: Dry 1 2 3 4 5 6 7 8 9 10 Sweet

Body: Light Light to Medium Medium Medium to Full Full

Balance: Unbalanced 1 2 3 4 5 6 7 8 9 10 Balanced

Finish: Short Short to Medium Medium Medium to Long Long

Overall Tasting Experience: Poor 1 2 3 4 5 6 7 8 9 10 Excellent

Price-to-Value Ratio: Poor 1 2 3 4 5 6 7 8 9 10 Excellent

Aromas and Tastes: _____

_____

Comments on Vintage, Region, Winemaker: _____

_____

Recommended   Not Recommended

(Circle One)

WINE: _____ Vintage: _____ Producer: _____

Region/Country: _____ Price: _____ Date Tasted: _____

Grape(s): _____

Importer/Distributor: _____ Alcohol % _____

CIRCLE YOUR RATINGS BELOW.

Color/Style: Red   White   Rosé   Sparkling   Effervescent   Fortified

Appearance: Thin   Translucent   Saturated   Opaque

Dry/Sweet Spectrum: Dry   1   2   3   4   5   6   7   8   9   10   Sweet

Body: Light   Light to Medium   Medium   Medium to Full   Full

Balance: Unbalanced   1   2   3   4   5   6   7   8   9   10   Balanced

Finish: Short   Short to Medium   Medium   Medium to Long   Long

Overall Tasting Experience: Poor   1   2   3   4   5   6   7   8   9   10   Excellent

Price-to-Value Ratio: Poor   1   2   3   4   5   6   7   8   9   10   Excellent

Aromas and Tastes: _____

_____

Comments on Vintage, Region, Winemaker: _____

_____

Recommended	Not Recommended
(Circle One)	

WINE: _____ Vintage: _____ Producer: _____

Region/Country: _____ Price: _____ Date Tasted: _____

Grape(s): _____

Importer/Distributor: _____ Alcohol % _____

CIRCLE YOUR RATINGS BELOW.

Color/Style: Red   White   Rosé   Sparkling   Effervescent   Fortified

Appearance: Thin   Translucent   Saturated   Opaque

Dry/Sweet Spectrum: Dry   1   2   3   4   5   6   7   8   9   10   Sweet

Body: Light   Light to Medium   Medium   Medium to Full   Full

Balance: Unbalanced   1   2   3   4   5   6   7   8   9   10   Balanced

Finish: Short   Short to Medium   Medium   Medium to Long   Long

Overall Tasting Experience: Poor   1   2   3   4   5   6   7   8   9   10   Excellent

Price-to-Value Ratio: Poor   1   2   3   4   5   6   7   8   9   10   Excellent

Aromas and Tastes: _____

_____

Comments on Vintage, Region, Winemaker: _____

_____

Recommended   Not Recommended
              (*Circle One*)

WINE: _____ Vintage: _____ Producer: _____

Region/Country: _____ Price: _____ Date Tasted: _____

Grape(s): _____

Importer/Distributor: _____ Alcohol % _____

CIRCLE YOUR RATINGS BELOW.

Color/Style: Red White Rosé Sparkling Effervescent Fortified

Appearance: Thin Translucent Saturated Opaque

Dry/Sweet Spectrum: Dry 1 2 3 4 5 6 7 8 9 10 Sweet

Body: Light Light to Medium Medium Medium to Full Full

Balance: Unbalanced 1 2 3 4 5 6 7 8 9 10 Balanced

Finish: Short Short to Medium Medium Medium to Long Long

Overall Tasting Experience: Poor 1 2 3 4 5 6 7 8 9 10 Excellent

Price-to-Value Ratio: Poor 1 2 3 4 5 6 7 8 9 10 Excellent

Aromas and Tastes: _____

_____

Comments on Vintage, Region, Winemaker: _____

_____

Recommended	Not Recommended
	(*Circle One*)

WINE: _____ Vintage: _____ Producer: _____

Region/Country: _____ Price: _____ Date Tasted: _____

Grape(s): _____

Importer/Distributor: _____ Alcohol % _____

CIRCLE YOUR RATINGS BELOW.

Color/Style: Red   White   Rosé   Sparkling   Effervescent   Fortified

Appearance: Thin   Translucent   Saturated   Opaque

Dry/Sweet Spectrum: Dry   1   2   3   4   5   6   7   8   9   10   Sweet

Body: Light   Light to Medium   Medium   Medium to Full   Full

Balance: Unbalanced   1   2   3   4   5   6   7   8   9   10   Balanced

Finish: Short   Short to Medium   Medium   Medium to Long   Long

Overall Tasting Experience: Poor   1   2   3   4   5   6   7   8   9   10   Excellent

Price-to-Value Ratio: Poor   1   2   3   4   5   6   7   8   9   10   Excellent

Aromas and Tastes: _____

_____

Comments on Vintage, Region, Winemaker: _____

_____

Recommended   Not Recommended

(Circle One)

WINE: _____ Vintage: _____ Producer: _____

Region/Country: _____ Price: _____ Date Tasted: _____

Grape(s): _____

Importer/Distributor: _____ Alcohol % _____

CIRCLE YOUR RATINGS BELOW.

Color/Style: Red   White   Rosé   Sparkling   Effervescent   Fortified

Appearance: Thin   Translucent   Saturated   Opaque

Dry/Sweet Spectrum: Dry   1   2   3   4   5   6   7   8   9   10   Sweet

Body: Light   Light to Medium   Medium   Medium to Full   Full

Balance: Unbalanced   1   2   3   4   5   6   7   8   9   10   Balanced

Finish: Short   Short to Medium   Medium   Medium to Long   Long

Overall Tasting Experience: Poor   1   2   3   4   5   6   7   8   9   10   Excellent

Price-to-Value Ratio: Poor   1   2   3   4   5   6   7   8   9   10   Excellent

Aromas and Tastes: _____

_____

Comments on Vintage, Region, Winemaker: _____

_____

Recommended	Not Recommended
	(Circle One)	

WINE: _____ Vintage: _____ Producer: _____

Region/Country: _____ Price: _____ Date Tasted: _____

Grape(s): _____

Importer/Distributor: _____ Alcohol % _____

CIRCLE YOUR RATINGS BELOW.

Color/Style: Red White Rosé Sparkling Effervescent Fortified

Appearance: Thin Translucent Saturated Opaque

Dry/Sweet Spectrum: Dry 1 2 3 4 5 6 7 8 9 10 Sweet

Body: Light Light to Medium Medium Medium to Full Full

Balance: Unbalanced 1 2 3 4 5 6 7 8 9 10 Balanced

Finish: Short Short to Medium Medium Medium to Long Long

Overall Tasting Experience: Poor 1 2 3 4 5 6 7 8 9 10 Excellent

Price-to-Value Ratio: Poor 1 2 3 4 5 6 7 8 9 10 Excellent

Aromas and Tastes: _____

_____

Comments on Vintage, Region, Winemaker: _____

_____

Recommended   Not Recommended

(*Circle One*)

WINE: _____ Vintage: _____ Producer: _____

Region/Country: _____ Price: _____ Date Tasted: _____

Grape(s): _____

Importer/Distributor: _____ Alcohol % _____

CIRCLE YOUR RATINGS BELOW.

Color/Style: Red   White   Rosé   Sparkling   Effervescent   Fortified

Appearance: Thin   Translucent   Saturated   Opaque

Dry/Sweet Spectrum: Dry   1   2   3   4   5   6   7   8   9   10   Sweet

Body: Light   Light to Medium   Medium   Medium to Full   Full

Balance: Unbalanced   1   2   3   4   5   6   7   8   9   10   Balanced

Finish: Short   Short to Medium   Medium   Medium to Long   Long

Overall Tasting Experience: Poor   1   2   3   4   5   6   7   8   9   10   Excellent

Price-to-Value Ratio: Poor   1   2   3   4   5   6   7   8   9   10   Excellent

Aromas and Tastes: _____

_____

Comments on Vintage, Region, Winemaker: _____

_____

Recommended	Not Recommended

(*Circle One*)

WINE: _____ Vintage: _____ Producer: _____

Region/Country: _____ Price: _____ Date Tasted: _____

Grape(s): _____

Importer/Distributor: _____ Alcohol % _____

CIRCLE YOUR RATINGS BELOW.

Color/Style: Red White Rosé Sparkling Effervescent Fortified

Appearance: Thin Translucent Saturated Opaque

Dry/Sweet Spectrum: Dry 1 2 3 4 5 6 7 8 9 10 Sweet

Body: Light Light to Medium Medium Medium to Full Full

Balance: Unbalanced 1 2 3 4 5 6 7 8 9 10 Balanced

Finish: Short Short to Medium Medium Medium to Long Long

Overall Tasting Experience: Poor 1 2 3 4 5 6 7 8 9 10 Excellent

Price-to-Value Ratio: Poor 1 2 3 4 5 6 7 8 9 10 Excellent

Aromas and Tastes: _____

_____

Comments on Vintage, Region, Winemaker: _____

_____

Recommended   Not Recommended
                        (Circle One)

WINE: _____ Vintage: _____ Producer: _____

Region/Country: _____ Price: _____ Date Tasted: _____

Grape(s): _____

Importer/Distributor: _____ Alcohol % _____

CIRCLE YOUR RATINGS BELOW.

Color/Style: Red White Rosé Sparkling Effervescent Fortified

Appearance: Thin Translucent Saturated Opaque

Dry/Sweet Spectrum: Dry 1 2 3 4 5 6 7 8 9 10 Sweet

Body: Light Light to Medium Medium Medium to Full Full

Balance: Unbalanced 1 2 3 4 5 6 7 8 9 10 Balanced

Finish: Short Short to Medium Medium Medium to Long Long

Overall Tasting Experience: Poor 1 2 3 4 5 6 7 8 9 10 Excellent

Price-to-Value Ratio: Poor 1 2 3 4 5 6 7 8 9 10 Excellent

Aromas and Tastes: _____

_____

Comments on Vintage, Region, Winemaker: _____

_____

Recommended	Not Recommended
	(Circle One)	

163

WINE: _____ Vintage: _____ Producer: _____

Region/Country: _____ Price: _____ Date Tasted: _____

Grape(s): _____

Importer/Distributor: _____ Alcohol % _____

CIRCLE YOUR RATINGS BELOW.

Color/Style: Red White Rosé Sparkling Effervescent Fortified

Appearance: Thin Translucent Saturated Opaque

Dry/Sweet Spectrum: Dry 1 2 3 4 5 6 7 8 9 10 Sweet

Body: Light Light to Medium Medium Medium to Full Full

Balance: Unbalanced 1 2 3 4 5 6 7 8 9 10 Balanced

Finish: Short Short to Medium Medium Medium to Long Long

Overall Tasting Experience: Poor 1 2 3 4 5 6 7 8 9 10 Excellent

Price-to-Value Ratio: Poor 1 2 3 4 5 6 7 8 9 10 Excellent

Aromas and Tastes: _____

_____

Comments on Vintage, Region, Winemaker: _____

_____

Recommended		Not Recommended
	(Circle One)	

WINE: _____ Vintage: _____ Producer: _____

Region/Country: _____ Price: _____ Date Tasted: _____

Grape(s): _____

Importer/Distributor: _____ Alcohol % _____

CIRCLE YOUR RATINGS BELOW.

Color/Style: Red   White   Rosé   Sparkling   Effervescent   Fortified

Appearance: Thin   Translucent   Saturated   Opaque

Dry/Sweet Spectrum: Dry   1   2   3   4   5   6   7   8   9   10   Sweet

Body: Light   Light to Medium   Medium   Medium to Full   Full

Balance: Unbalanced   1   2   3   4   5   6   7   8   9   10   Balanced

Finish: Short   Short to Medium   Medium   Medium to Long   Long

Overall Tasting Experience: Poor   1   2   3   4   5   6   7   8   9   10   Excellent

Price-to-Value Ratio: Poor   1   2   3   4   5   6   7   8   9   10   Excellent

Aromas and Tastes: _____

_____

Comments on Vintage, Region, Winemaker: _____

_____

Recommended   Not Recommended
                (*Circle One*)

WINE: _____ Vintage: _____ Producer: _____

Region/Country: _____ Price: _____ Date Tasted: _____

Grape(s): _____

Importer/Distributor: _____ Alcohol % _____

CIRCLE YOUR RATINGS BELOW.

Color/Style: Red White Rosé Sparkling Effervescent Fortified

Appearance: Thin Translucent Saturated Opaque

Dry/Sweet Spectrum: Dry 1 2 3 4 5 6 7 8 9 10 Sweet

Body: Light Light to Medium Medium Medium to Full Full

Balance: Unbalanced 1 2 3 4 5 6 7 8 9 10 Balanced

Finish: Short Short to Medium Medium Medium to Long Long

Overall Tasting Experience: Poor 1 2 3 4 5 6 7 8 9 10 Excellent

Price-to-Value Ratio: Poor 1 2 3 4 5 6 7 8 9 10 Excellent

Aromas and Tastes: _____

_____

Comments on Vintage, Region, Winemaker: _____

_____

Recommended   Not Recommended
                 (*Circle One*)

166

WINE: _____ Vintage: _____ Producer: _____

Region/Country: _____ Price: _____ Date Tasted: _____

Grape(s): _____

Importer/Distributor: _____ Alcohol % _____

CIRCLE YOUR RATINGS BELOW.

Color/Style: Red   White   Rosé   Sparkling   Effervescent   Fortified

Appearance: Thin   Translucent   Saturated   Opaque

Dry/Sweet Spectrum: Dry   1   2   3   4   5   6   7   8   9   10   Sweet

Body: Light   Light to Medium   Medium   Medium to Full   Full

Balance: Unbalanced   1   2   3   4   5   6   7   8   9   10   Balanced

Finish: Short   Short to Medium   Medium   Medium to Long   Long

Overall Tasting Experience: Poor   1   2   3   4   5   6   7   8   9   10   Excellent

Price-to-Value Ratio: Poor   1   2   3   4   5   6   7   8   9   10   Excellent

Aromas and Tastes: _____

_____

Comments on Vintage, Region, Winemaker: _____

_____

Recommended		Not Recommended
	(Circle One)	

WINE: _____ Vintage: _____ Producer: _____

Region/Country: _____ Price: _____ Date Tasted: _____

Grape(s): _____

Importer/Distributor: _____ Alcohol % _____

CIRCLE YOUR RATINGS BELOW.

Color/Style: Red White Rosé Sparkling Effervescent Fortified

Appearance: Thin Translucent Saturated Opaque

Dry/Sweet Spectrum: Dry 1 2 3 4 5 6 7 8 9 10 Sweet

Body: Light Light to Medium Medium Medium to Full Full

Balance: Unbalanced 1 2 3 4 5 6 7 8 9 10 Balanced

Finish: Short Short to Medium Medium Medium to Long Long

Overall Tasting Experience: Poor 1 2 3 4 5 6 7 8 9 10 Excellent

Price-to-Value Ratio: Poor 1 2 3 4 5 6 7 8 9 10 Excellent

Aromas and Tastes: _____

_____

Comments on Vintage, Region, Winemaker: _____

_____

Recommended	Not Recommended
	(Circle One)	

WINE: _____ Vintage: _____ Producer: _____

Region/Country: _____ Price: _____ Date Tasted: _____

Grape(s): _____

Importer/Distributor: _____ Alcohol % _____

CIRCLE YOUR RATINGS BELOW.

Color/Style: Red   White   Rosé   Sparkling   Effervescent   Fortified

Appearance: Thin   Translucent   Saturated   Opaque

Dry/Sweet Spectrum: Dry   1   2   3   4   5   6   7   8   9   10   Sweet

Body: Light   Light to Medium   Medium   Medium to Full   Full

Balance: Unbalanced   1   2   3   4   5   6   7   8   9   10   Balanced

Finish: Short   Short to Medium   Medium   Medium to Long   Long

Overall Tasting Experience: Poor   1   2   3   4   5   6   7   8   9   10   Excellent

Price-to-Value Ratio: Poor   1   2   3   4   5   6   7   8   9   10   Excellent

Aromas and Tastes: _____

_____

Comments on Vintage, Region, Winemaker: _____

_____

Recommended		Not Recommended
	(Circle One)	

169

WINE: _____ Vintage: _____ Producer: _____

Region/Country: _____ Price: _____ Date Tasted: _____

Grape(s): _____

Importer/Distributor: _____ Alcohol % _____

CIRCLE YOUR RATINGS BELOW.

Color/Style: Red   White   Rosé   Sparkling   Effervescent   Fortified

Appearance: Thin   Translucent   Saturated   Opaque

Dry/Sweet Spectrum: Dry   1   2   3   4   5   6   7   8   9   10   Sweet

Body: Light   Light to Medium   Medium   Medium to Full   Full

Balance: Unbalanced   1   2   3   4   5   6   7   8   9   10   Balanced

Finish: Short   Short to Medium   Medium   Medium to Long   Long

Overall Tasting Experience: Poor   1   2   3   4   5   6   7   8   9   10   Excellent

Price-to-Value Ratio: Poor   1   2   3   4   5   6   7   8   9   10   Excellent

Aromas and Tastes: _____

_____

Comments on Vintage, Region, Winemaker: _____

_____

Recommended   Not Recommended
                    (Circle One)

WINE: _____ Vintage: _____ Producer: _____

Region/Country: _____ Price: _____ Date Tasted: _____

Grape(s): _____

Importer/Distributor: _____ Alcohol % _____

CIRCLE YOUR RATINGS BELOW.

Color/Style: Red   White   Rosé   Sparkling   Effervescent   Fortified

Appearance: Thin   Translucent   Saturated   Opaque

Dry/Sweet Spectrum: Dry   1   2   3   4   5   6   7   8   9   10   Sweet

Body: Light   Light to Medium   Medium   Medium to Full   Full

Balance: Unbalanced   1   2   3   4   5   6   7   8   9   10   Balanced

Finish: Short   Short to Medium   Medium   Medium to Long   Long

Overall Tasting Experience: Poor   1   2   3   4   5   6   7   8   9   10   Excellent

Price-to-Value Ratio: Poor   1   2   3   4   5   6   7   8   9   10   Excellent

Aromas and Tastes: _____

_____

Comments on Vintage, Region, Winemaker: _____

_____

Recommended	Not Recommended

(Circle One)

WINE: _____ Vintage: _____ Producer: _____

Region/Country: _____ Price: _____ Date Tasted: _____

Grape(s): _____

Importer/Distributor: _____ Alcohol % _____

CIRCLE YOUR RATINGS BELOW.

Color/Style: Red White Rosé Sparkling Effervescent Fortified

Appearance: Thin Translucent Saturated Opaque

Dry/Sweet Spectrum: Dry 1 2 3 4 5 6 7 8 9 10 Sweet

Body: Light Light to Medium Medium Medium to Full Full

Balance: Unbalanced 1 2 3 4 5 6 7 8 9 10 Balanced

Finish: Short Short to Medium Medium Medium to Long Long

Overall Tasting Experience: Poor 1 2 3 4 5 6 7 8 9 10 Excellent

Price-to-Value Ratio: Poor 1 2 3 4 5 6 7 8 9 10 Excellent

Aromas and Tastes: _____

_____

Comments on Vintage, Region, Winemaker: _____

_____

Recommended   Not Recommended
                  (*Circle One*)

WINE: _____ Vintage: _____ Producer: _____

Region/Country: _____ Price: _____ Date Tasted: _____

Grape(s): _____

Importer/Distributor: _____ Alcohol % _____

CIRCLE YOUR RATINGS BELOW.

Color/Style: Red White Rosé Sparkling Effervescent Fortified

Appearance: Thin Translucent Saturated Opaque

Dry/Sweet Spectrum: Dry 1 2 3 4 5 6 7 8 9 10 Sweet

Body: Light Light to Medium Medium Medium to Full Full

Balance: Unbalanced 1 2 3 4 5 6 7 8 9 10 Balanced

Finish: Short Short to Medium Medium Medium to Long Long

Overall Tasting Experience: Poor 1 2 3 4 5 6 7 8 9 10 Excellent

Price-to-Value Ratio: Poor 1 2 3 4 5 6 7 8 9 10 Excellent

Aromas and Tastes: _____

_____

Comments on Vintage, Region, Winemaker: _____

_____

Recommended   Not Recommended
                    (*Circle One*)

WINE: _____ Vintage: _____ Producer: _____

Region/Country: _____ Price: _____ Date Tasted: _____

Grape(s): _____

Importer/Distributor: _____ Alcohol % _____

CIRCLE YOUR RATINGS BELOW.

Color/Style: Red White Rosé Sparkling Effervescent Fortified

Appearance: Thin Translucent Saturated Opaque

Dry/Sweet Spectrum: Dry 1 2 3 4 5 6 7 8 9 10 Sweet

Body: Light Light to Medium Medium Medium to Full Full

Balance: Unbalanced 1 2 3 4 5 6 7 8 9 10 Balanced

Finish: Short Short to Medium Medium Medium to Long Long

Overall Tasting Experience: Poor 1 2 3 4 5 6 7 8 9 10 Excellent

Price-to-Value Ratio: Poor 1 2 3 4 5 6 7 8 9 10 Excellent

Aromas and Tastes: _____

_____

Comments on Vintage, Region, Winemaker: _____

.

_____

Recommended   Not Recommended
                (*Circle One*)

WINE: .... Vintage: .... Producer: ....

Region/Country: .... Price: .... Date Tasted: ....

Grape(s): ....

Importer/Distributor: .... Alcohol % ....

CIRCLE YOUR RATINGS BELOW.

Color/Style: Red White Rosé Sparkling Effervescent Fortified

Appearance: Thin Translucent Saturated Opaque

Dry/Sweet Spectrum: Dry 1 2 3 4 5 6 7 8 9 10 Sweet

Body: Light Light to Medium Medium Medium to Full Full

Balance: Unbalanced 1 2 3 4 5 6 7 8 9 10 Balanced

Finish: Short Short to Medium Medium Medium to Long Long

Overall Tasting Experience: Poor 1 2 3 4 5 6 7 8 9 10 Excellent

Price-to-Value Ratio: Poor 1 2 3 4 5 6 7 8 9 10 Excellent

Aromas and Tastes: ....

....

Comments on Vintage, Region, Winemaker: ....

....

Recommended   Not Recommended
(*Circle One*)

WINE: _____ Vintage: _____ Producer: _____

Region/Country: _____ Price: _____ Date Tasted: _____

Grape(s): _____

Importer/Distributor: _____ Alcohol % _____

CIRCLE YOUR RATINGS BELOW.

Color/Style: Red White Rosé Sparkling Effervescent Fortified

Appearance: Thin Translucent Saturated Opaque

Dry/Sweet Spectrum: Dry 1 2 3 4 5 6 7 8 9 10 Sweet

Body: Light Light to Medium Medium Medium to Full Full

Balance: Unbalanced 1 2 3 4 5 6 7 8 9 10 Balanced

Finish: Short Short to Medium Medium Medium to Long Long

Overall Tasting Experience: Poor 1 2 3 4 5 6 7 8 9 10 Excellent

Price-to-Value Ratio: Poor 1 2 3 4 5 6 7 8 9 10 Excellent

Aromas and Tastes: _____

_____

Comments on Vintage, Region, Winemaker: _____

_____

Recommended	Not Recommended
	(Circle One)	

WINE: _____ Vintage: _____ Producer: _____

Region/Country: _____ Price: _____ Date Tasted: _____

Grape(s): _____

Importer/Distributor: _____ Alcohol % _____

CIRCLE YOUR RATINGS BELOW.

Color/Style: Red   White   Rosé   Sparkling   Effervescent   Fortified

Appearance: Thin   Translucent   Saturated   Opaque

Dry/Sweet Spectrum: Dry   1   2   3   4   5   6   7   8   9   10   Sweet

Body: Light   Light to Medium   Medium   Medium to Full   Full

Balance: Unbalanced   1   2   3   4   5   6   7   8   9   10   Balanced

Finish: Short   Short to Medium   Medium   Medium to Long   Long

Overall Tasting Experience: Poor   1   2   3   4   5   6   7   8   9   10   Excellent

Price-to-Value Ratio: Poor   1   2   3   4   5   6   7   8   9   10   Excellent

Aromas and Tastes: _____

_____

Comments on Vintage, Region, Winemaker: _____

_____

Recommended   Not Recommended

(Circle One)

WINE: _____ Vintage: _____ Producer: _____

Region/Country: _____ Price: _____ Date Tasted: _____

Grape(s): _____

Importer/Distributor: _____ Alcohol % _____

CIRCLE YOUR RATINGS BELOW.

Color/Style: Red White Rosé Sparkling Effervescent Fortified

Appearance: Thin Translucent Saturated Opaque

Dry/Sweet Spectrum: Dry 1 2 3 4 5 6 7 8 9 10 Sweet

Body: Light Light to Medium Medium Medium to Full Full

Balance: Unbalanced 1 2 3 4 5 6 7 8 9 10 Balanced

Finish: Short Short to Medium Medium Medium to Long Long

Overall Tasting Experience: Poor 1 2 3 4 5 6 7 8 9 10 Excellent

Price-to-Value Ratio: Poor 1 2 3 4 5 6 7 8 9 10 Excellent

Aromas and Tastes: _____

_____

Comments on Vintage, Region, Winemaker: _____

_____

Recommended   Not Recommended

(Circle One)

WINE: _____ Vintage: _____ Producer: _____

Region/Country: _____ Price: _____ Date Tasted: _____

Grape(s): _____

Importer/Distributor: _____ Alcohol % _____

CIRCLE YOUR RATINGS BELOW.

Color/Style: Red   White   Rosé   Sparkling   Effervescent   Fortified

Appearance: Thin   Translucent   Saturated   Opaque

Dry/Sweet Spectrum: Dry   1   2   3   4   5   6   7   8   9   10   Sweet

Body: Light   Light to Medium   Medium   Medium to Full   Full

Balance: Unbalanced   1   2   3   4   5   6   7   8   9   10   Balanced

Finish: Short   Short to Medium   Medium   Medium to Long   Long

Overall Tasting Experience: Poor   1   2   3   4   5   6   7   8   9   10   Excellent

Price-to-Value Ratio: Poor   1   2   3   4   5   6   7   8   9   10   Excellent

Aromas and Tastes: _____

_____

Comments on Vintage, Region, Winemaker: _____

_____

Recommended		Not Recommended
	(Circle One)	

WINE: _____ Vintage: _____ Producer: _____

Region/Country: _____ Price: _____ Date Tasted: _____

Grape(s): _____

Importer/Distributor: _____ Alcohol % _____

CIRCLE YOUR RATINGS BELOW.

Color/Style: Red White Rosé Sparkling Effervescent Fortified

Appearance: Thin Translucent Saturated Opaque

Dry/Sweet Spectrum: Dry 1 2 3 4 5 6 7 8 9 10 Sweet

Body: Light Light to Medium Medium Medium to Full Full

Balance: Unbalanced 1 2 3 4 5 6 7 8 9 10 Balanced

Finish: Short Short to Medium Medium Medium to Long Long

Overall Tasting Experience: Poor 1 2 3 4 5 6 7 8 9 10 Excellent

Price-to-Value Ratio: Poor 1 2 3 4 5 6 7 8 9 10 Excellent

Aromas and Tastes: _____

_____

Comments on Vintage, Region, Winemaker: _____

_____

Recommended	Not Recommended
	(Circle One)

WINE:_____ Vintage:_____ Producer:_____

Region/Country:_____ Price:_____ Date Tasted:_____

Grape(s):_____

Importer/Distributor:_____ Alcohol %_____

CIRCLE YOUR RATINGS BELOW.

Color/Style: Red   White   Rosé   Sparkling   Effervescent   Fortified

Appearance: Thin   Translucent   Saturated   Opaque

Dry/Sweet Spectrum: Dry   1   2   3   4   5   6   7   8   9   10   Sweet

Body: Light   Light to Medium   Medium   Medium to Full   Full

Balance: Unbalanced   1   2   3   4   5   6   7   8   9   10   Balanced

Finish: Short   Short to Medium   Medium   Medium to Long   Long

Overall Tasting Experience: Poor   1   2   3   4   5   6   7   8   9   10   Excellent

Price-to-Value Ratio: Poor   1   2   3   4   5   6   7   8   9   10   Excellent

Aromas and Tastes:_____

_____

Comments on Vintage, Region, Winemaker:_____

_____

Recommended	Not Recommended

(Circle One)

181

WINE: _____ Vintage: _____ Producer: _____

Region/Country: _____ Price: _____ Date Tasted: _____

Grape(s): _____

Importer/Distributor: _____ Alcohol % _____

CIRCLE YOUR RATINGS BELOW.

Color/Style: Red   White   Rosé   Sparkling   Effervescent   Fortified

Appearance: Thin   Translucent   Saturated   Opaque

Dry/Sweet Spectrum: Dry   1   2   3   4   5   6   7   8   9   10   Sweet

Body: Light   Light to Medium   Medium   Medium to Full   Full

Balance: Unbalanced   1   2   3   4   5   6   7   8   9   10   Balanced

Finish: Short   Short to Medium   Medium   Medium to Long   Long

Overall Tasting Experience: Poor   1   2   3   4   5   6   7   8   9   10   Excellent

Price-to-Value Ratio: Poor   1   2   3   4   5   6   7   8   9   10   Excellent

Aromas and Tastes: _____

_____

Comments on Vintage, Region, Winemaker: _____

_____

Recommended		Not Recommended
	(Circle One)	

WINE: _____ Vintage: _____ Producer: _____

Region/Country: _____ Price: _____ Date Tasted: _____

Grape(s): _____

Importer/Distributor: _____ Alcohol % _____

CIRCLE YOUR RATINGS BELOW.

Color/Style: Red White Rosé Sparkling Effervescent Fortified

Appearance: Thin Translucent Saturated Opaque

Dry/Sweet Spectrum: Dry 1 2 3 4 5 6 7 8 9 10 Sweet

Body: Light Light to Medium Medium Medium to Full Full

Balance: Unbalanced 1 2 3 4 5 6 7 8 9 10 Balanced

Finish: Short Short to Medium Medium Medium to Long Long

Overall Tasting Experience: Poor 1 2 3 4 5 6 7 8 9 10 Excellent

Price-to-Value Ratio: Poor 1 2 3 4 5 6 7 8 9 10 Excellent

Aromas and Tastes: _____

_____

Comments on Vintage, Region, Winemaker: _____

_____

Recommended   Not Recommended
              (Circle One)

WINE:		Vintage:	Producer:

Region/Country: _____ Price: _____ Date Tasted: _____

Grape(s): _____

Importer/Distributor: _____ Alcohol % _____

CIRCLE YOUR RATINGS BELOW.

Color/Style: Red White Rosé Sparkling Effervescent Fortified

Appearance: Thin Translucent Saturated Opaque

Dry/Sweet Spectrum: Dry 1 2 3 4 5 6 7 8 9 10 Sweet

Body: Light Light to Medium Medium Medium to Full Full

Balance: Unbalanced 1 2 3 4 5 6 7 8 9 10 Balanced

Finish: Short Short to Medium Medium Medium to Long Long

Overall Tasting Experience: Poor 1 2 3 4 5 6 7 8 9 10 Excellent

Price-to-Value Ratio: Poor 1 2 3 4 5 6 7 8 9 10 Excellent

Aromas and Tastes: _____

_____

Comments on Vintage, Region, Winemaker: _____

_____

Recommended   Not Recommended

(Circle One)

WINE: _____ Vintage: _____ Producer: _____

Region/Country: _____ Price: _____ Date Tasted: _____

Grape(s): _____

Importer/Distributor: _____ Alcohol % _____

CIRCLE YOUR RATINGS BELOW.

Color/Style: Red   White   Rosé   Sparkling   Effervescent   Fortified

Appearance: Thin   Translucent   Saturated   Opaque

Dry/Sweet Spectrum: Dry   1   2   3   4   5   6   7   8   9   10   Sweet

Body: Light   Light to Medium   Medium   Medium to Full   Full

Balance: Unbalanced   1   2   3   4   5   6   7   8   9   10   Balanced

Finish: Short   Short to Medium   Medium   Medium to Long   Long

Overall Tasting Experience: Poor   1   2   3   4   5   6   7   8   9   10   Excellent

Price-to-Value Ratio: Poor   1   2   3   4   5   6   7   8   9   10   Excellent

Aromas and Tastes: _____

_____

Comments on Vintage, Region, Winemaker: _____

_____

Recommended	Not Recommended
	(Circle One)

185

WINE: _____ Vintage: _____ Producer: _____

Region/Country: _____ Price: _____ Date Tasted: _____

Grape(s): _____

Importer/Distributor: _____ Alcohol % _____

CIRCLE YOUR RATINGS BELOW.

Color/Style: Red   White   Rosé   Sparkling   Effervescent   Fortified

Appearance: Thin   Translucent   Saturated   Opaque

Dry/Sweet Spectrum: Dry   1   2   3   4   5   6   7   8   9   10   Sweet

Body: Light   Light to Medium   Medium   Medium to Full   Full

Balance: Unbalanced   1   2   3   4   5   6   7   8   9   10   Balanced

Finish: Short   Short to Medium   Medium   Medium to Long   Long

Overall Tasting Experience: Poor   1   2   3   4   5   6   7   8   9   10   Excellent

Price-to-Value Ratio: Poor   1   2   3   4   5   6   7   8   9   10   Excellent

Aromas and Tastes: _____

_____

Comments on Vintage, Region, Winemaker: _____

_____

Recommended   Not Recommended
                    (Circle One)

WINE: _____ Vintage: _____ Producer: _____

Region/Country: _____ Price: _____ Date Tasted: _____

Grape(s): _____

Importer/Distributor: _____ Alcohol % _____

CIRCLE YOUR RATINGS BELOW.

Color/Style: Red   White   Rosé   Sparkling   Effervescent   Fortified

Appearance: Thin   Translucent   Saturated   Opaque

Dry/Sweet Spectrum: Dry   1   2   3   4   5   6   7   8   9   10   Sweet

Body: Light   Light to Medium   Medium   Medium to Full   Full

Balance: Unbalanced   1   2   3   4   5   6   7   8   9   10   Balanced

Finish: Short   Short to Medium   Medium   Medium to Long   Long

Overall Tasting Experience: Poor   1   2   3   4   5   6   7   8   9   10   Excellent

Price-to-Value Ratio: Poor   1   2   3   4   5   6   7   8   9   10   Excellent

Aromas and Tastes: _____

_____

Comments on Vintage, Region, Winemaker: _____

_____

Recommended		Not Recommended
	(Circle One)	

187

WINE: _____ Vintage: _____ Producer: _____

Region/Country: _____ Price: _____ Date Tasted: _____

Grape(s): _____

Importer/Distributor: _____ Alcohol % _____

CIRCLE YOUR RATINGS BELOW.

Color/Style: Red White Rosé Sparkling Effervescent Fortified

Appearance: Thin Translucent Saturated Opaque

Dry/Sweet Spectrum: Dry 1 2 3 4 5 6 7 8 9 10 Sweet

Body: Light Light to Medium Medium Medium to Full Full

Balance: Unbalanced 1 2 3 4 5 6 7 8 9 10 Balanced

Finish: Short Short to Medium Medium Medium to Long Long

Overall Tasting Experience: Poor 1 2 3 4 5 6 7 8 9 10 Excellent

Price-to-Value Ratio: Poor 1 2 3 4 5 6 7 8 9 10 Excellent

Aromas and Tastes: _____

_____

Comments on Vintage, Region, Winemaker: _____

_____

Recommended   Not Recommended

(Circle One)

WINE: _____ Vintage: _____ Producer: _____

Region/Country: _____ Price: _____ Date Tasted: _____

Grape(s): _____

Importer/Distributor: _____ Alcohol % _____

CIRCLE YOUR RATINGS BELOW.

Color/Style: Red   White   Rosé   Sparkling   Effervescent   Fortified

Appearance: Thin   Translucent   Saturated   Opaque

Dry/Sweet Spectrum: Dry   1   2   3   4   5   6   7   8   9   10   Sweet

Body: Light   Light to Medium   Medium   Medium to Full   Full

Balance: Unbalanced   1   2   3   4   5   6   7   8   9   10   Balanced

Finish: Short   Short to Medium   Medium   Medium to Long   Long

Overall Tasting Experience: Poor   1   2   3   4   5   6   7   8   9   10   Excellent

Price-to-Value Ratio: Poor   1   2   3   4   5   6   7   8   9   10   Excellent

Aromas and Tastes: _____

_____

Comments on Vintage, Region, Winemaker: _____

_____

Recommended		Not Recommended
	(Circle One)	

WINE: _____ Vintage: _____ Producer: _____

Region/Country: _____ Price: _____ Date Tasted: _____

Grape(s): _____

Importer/Distributor: _____ Alcohol % _____

CIRCLE YOUR RATINGS BELOW.

Color/Style: Red White Rosé Sparkling Effervescent Fortified

Appearance: Thin Translucent Saturated Opaque

Dry/Sweet Spectrum: Dry 1 2 3 4 5 6 7 8 9 10 Sweet

Body: Light Light to Medium Medium Medium to Full Full

Balance: Unbalanced 1 2 3 4 5 6 7 8 9 10 Balanced

Finish: Short Short to Medium Medium Medium to Long Long

Overall Tasting Experience: Poor 1 2 3 4 5 6 7 8 9 10 Excellent

Price-to-Value Ratio: Poor 1 2 3 4 5 6 7 8 9 10 Excellent

Aromas and Tastes: _____

_____

Comments on Vintage, Region, Winemaker: _____

_____

Recommended		Not Recommended
	(Circle One)	

WINE: _____ Vintage: _____ Producer: _____

Region/Country: _____ Price: _____ Date Tasted: _____

Grape(s): _____

Importer/Distributor: _____ Alcohol % _____

CIRCLE YOUR RATINGS BELOW.

Color/Style: Red White Rosé Sparkling Effervescent Fortified

Appearance: Thin Translucent Saturated Opaque

Dry/Sweet Spectrum: Dry 1 2 3 4 5 6 7 8 9 10 Sweet

Body: Light Light to Medium Medium Medium to Full Full

Balance: Unbalanced 1 2 3 4 5 6 7 8 9 10 Balanced

Finish: Short Short to Medium Medium Medium to Long Long

Overall Tasting Experience: Poor 1 2 3 4 5 6 7 8 9 10 Excellent

Price-to-Value Ratio: Poor 1 2 3 4 5 6 7 8 9 10 Excellent

Aromas and Tastes: _____

_____

Comments on Vintage, Region, Winemaker: _____

_____

Recommended		Not Recommended
	(Circle One)	

ABOUT THE AUTHOR

My love of food, fine dining, wine, and spirits began as a 19-year-old on Nantucket. I landed a waitering job in a fine French restaurant, and lived in a large house with chefs, bartenders, sommeliers, and other waiters. Every night after work we would cook up, and open up, something and discuss it. Fast forward many years. After assembling a somewhat respectable wine cellar, I joined a wine-tasting group, then pursued a personal passion and participated in the Sommelier Society of America wine course. I returned to my roots, delivering wine/beverage service (part time) at the acclaimed Hemingway's Restaurant in Killington, Vermont. The owners introduced me to the publisher of *Santé Magazine*, and I began reviewing wines and spirits for publication, and covering wine and food events in New York City. I write a regular wine & spirits column for *Wag Magazine*, and write a wine blog at www.DougPaulding.com.

I travel extensively and have written on wines and spirits from all over the world, including the Languedoc-Roussillon and the Loire Valley in France, Spain, Portugal, Italy, Chile, Scotland, Israel, the Dominican Republic, the Pacific Northwest, Texas, and Nova Scotia, as well as countless day trips for food, wine, and spirits events. If it's made with inspiration and care, I am interested.

Doug Paulding, South Salem, New York • www.DougPaulding.com